TEXACO
Collector's Guide

Scott Benjamin and Wayne Henderson

Motorbooks International
Publishers & Wholesalers

First published in 1997 by Motorbooks International
Publishers & Wholesalers, 729 Prospect Avenue,
PO Box 1, Osceola, WI 54020-0001 USA

Library of Congress Cataloging-in-Publication Data
Benjamin, Scott.
    Texaco collector's guide/Scott Benjamin &
        Wayne Henderson.
        p. cm.
    Includes index.
    ISBN 0-7603-0291-X (pbk.: alk. paper)
    1. Texaco, inc.—Collectibles—Catalogs. 2.
    Service stations—Collectibles—United
States—Catalogs. I. Henderson, Wayne. II. Title.
TL153.B3924   1997
629.28'6'075—dc21   97-13149

On the front cover: With so many different items
available, it's no wonder Texaco is the favorite oil
company among petroliana collectors. Gas pump
globes, service station signs, oil cans, road maps, toys,
and trinkets are just a few of the objects that wear the
famous Texaco star.

On the frontispiece: Texaco's logo appeared
everywhere, including dinnerware used in corporate
lunchrooms around the world.

On the title page: The fireman's helmet image has
been used by Texaco since the 1930s when it was
developed to promote "Fire Chief" gasoline. These toy
helmets date from 1985.

On the back cover: A sampling of popular Texaco
collectibles, from the upper left: a set of Texaco
dishes, a pocket watch and knife, a circa 1915
chimney-cap gas pump globe, a flange sign from the
1930s, and various oil containers.

Designed by Todd Sauers

Printed in Hong Kong through World Print, Ltd.

CONTENTS

ACKNOWLEDGMENTS

We would like to give special thanks to Richard Eaves for allowing us to photograph his extensive Texaco collection. Many of the items shown in this book are from Richard's collection, and we could not have accomplished this project without his help and generosity.

We also thank Nick Cedar Photography and the other photograph contributors for providing beautiful illustrations and rare photographs.

Scott Benjamin and Wayne Henderson

INTRODUCTION

The Red Gas Pump

Walk into any Wal-Mart today and you will find "bargain-bin" framed art prints featuring numerous nostalgic scenes—barns, grain mills, blacksmith shops, and other images of days gone by. Look closely at the print showing a general store. Standing proudly out in front is technology of the day at it's finest—a gas pump. Invariably, the gas pump in these otherwise generic art prints is red. Always red. Often, if any logo image is in view, a single red star adorns the pump.

Repeated over and over, the red gas pump with the star on top was one of the most familiar sights on earth for much of this century. Often, it was the first "industrialization" that rural residents encountered the world over. The pumps are so much a part of the culture that their image immediately means gasoline. But why?

In the earliest years of this century, a marketing powerhouse roared out of Texas, away from its Gulf Coast birthplace, to fuel and lubricate the twentieth century. Only the great industrial colossus, Standard Oil, can claim more influence on the making of the twentieth century. But Standard was an industrial complex, with refineries, pipelines, rail cars, all the trappings of the "cast iron age" that was the nineteenth century. Texaco was different. It was, and remains, a marketer, geared to serve an ever-growing market for petroleum and its products. In the following pages, we will tell the Texaco story through documentation of the many items that were used to advertise and promote Texaco products through the years.

How To Use This Book For Reference

This book has been assembled in a format that readers should find easy to use.

Each chapter covers a specific group of products—Globes, Signs, Toys, etc. Every effort has been made to present the information in a similar manner from chapter to chapter; however, the nature of specific product groups requires more or less information, so those sections have been tailored accordingly. In general, item listings appear as follows:

Item Title—Years Used or Official Date—Rarity—Type or Size—Price Range
    Descriptive Text.

These are interpreted as follows:

Item Title: Simply the name commonly used by collectors to refer to the item.

Years Used or Official Date: For gas pumps, signs, and globes, this refers to the years that the item would have been placed in service in a new installation. In practice, many items remained in use long after they had been officially replaced. For cans, maps, toys, and trinkets, this refers to the years that the item was sold as new stock (for cans), published (for maps), or issued (for toys and trinkets).

Rarity: A numerical guide system interpreted as follows:

1—Very common item, regularly found in collector circles.

2—Common item, less regularly found but still available in collector circles.

3—Available, these items are more scarce and are thus harder for average collectors to find.

4—Rare or very rare item, very few known to exist, seldom offered for sale on the collector market.

5—Extremely rare or unique items of which ten or less are known.

6—Only one example known to exist.

7—Known only in old photos, absolutely none found among known collectors.

Type or Size: Simply the type, approximate dimensions, or capacity of the item. Single numerals indicate the diameter of round signs. Can sizes are listed by liquid content measurement. Globe abbreviations are interpreted as follows:

OPE—One piece etched globe.

OPB—One piece globe with a baked enamel finish.

OPC—One piece cast globe with raised or recessed details.

Glass or Gill—Glass body globe with glass inserts.

CAPCO—Plastic body globe manufactured by Cincinnati Advertising Products Company consisting of two plastic body halves assembled around glass (or rarely, plastic) lenses.

Price Range: The price (range) at which this item is commonly traded, in collector circles. The lower-end pricing is considered wholesale, among dealers; while the upper-end is considered retail, to the end owner. Both are considered good deals within their respective definitions.

Descriptive Text: Several common features are used in descriptive text. They are as follows:

• Texaco Logo: Unless used with a modifier (current, hexagon, etc.), always refers to the classic logo, circular outlined white field surrounding a red five-point star with a green "T" in the center and usually the word "TEXACO" superimposed across the upper point of the star.

• Black Border and White Border "T." On the classic Texaco logo, the "T" in the star is surrounded by either a black outline or a white outline that distinguishes it from the surrounding red star. Replacement of the black border with the white border was gradual, beginning in 1936 on identification signs and progressing through 1945 on smaller items.

• Quotation Marks (" "): Indicate type wording as it appeared on the item.

• Slash (/) Mark: Indicates wording preceding the slash is displayed above that following the slash.

Chapter 1

Overview of the Petroleum Collectibles Hobby

Thousands of people worldwide are involved in the petroleum collectibles hobby. Beginning in the 1940s, people began accumulating paper items, gas pump globes, and early gas pumps on a very limited basis. Only a very small number of collectors—propably less than 10—were active in this era. In the 1960s, antique car enthusiasts began to seek out interesting service station items to accent their car collections, and several began actively to build their collections of globes and gas pumps. The 1970s saw the first national-level interest in the hobby, with the introduction of reproduction items to restore gas pumps. By the late 1970s, several books were available on the hobby and the history of the petroleum marketing industry. The early 1980s saw the beginning of several regularly published periodicals dealing with petroleum collectibles, and by the mid-1980s more books and the first of the now-numerous regional swap meets were being held. The hobby's popularity exploded in about 1989, and hundreds of new collectors join in the fun every year.

Most areas of the country are within a day's drive of some regional, annual event. For further information on the hobby, on books available, or to subscribe to *Petroleum Collectibles Monthly*, contact:

Texaco collectibles run the gamut, from signs and cans to toys and dinner ware. *Richard Eaves Collection*

Neon advertising clocks have been manufactured with every image conceivable. This beautiful Texaco clock is part of the Richard Eaves collection.

Petroleum Collectibles Monthly
411 Forest Street
LaGrange, OH 44050
(440) 355–6608
(440) 355–4955 Fax

Petroleum Collectibles Basics

Whether you're new to the hobby, have been actively participating in it for years, or have only a casual interest, the following information summarizes the various groups of memorabilia, and discusses the collector market's interest in products within each group.

Texaco jewelry, for identification or award purposes, is highly prized by Texaco employees and collectors of Texaco memorabilia. Shown here are early Texaco cuff-links. *Richard Eaves Collection*

Product groups are listed in order of general popularity.

Signs
Signs are considered the most popular petroleum collectible items today. The earliest signs were lithographed tin, but by 1920 porcelain began to see extensive use in the petroleum industry. Plastics, introduced to the industry in 1947 and commonly used after 1960, are much less collectible than the earlier tin and porcelain items. Neon was never extensively used in the gasoline industry, but collectors have recently taken interest in the few neon signs available. Prices range from a mere $25 for a recent plastic item, to over $10,000 for the most decorative and artistic porcelain signs offered. Many reproductions are available, so be careful and know what you are buying. Texaco signs with unusual graphics are among the most

desirable items. At the other end of the spectrum, the Texaco Fire Chief pump signs are perhaps the most commonly found petroleum signs of any kind. Signs were the primary subject of another Benjamin and Henderson book, *Gas And Oil Signs*, published by Motorbooks International in 1996.

Globes
Second in popularity only to signs are gas pump globes. From the earliest one-piece, etched, milk glass domes, to the plastic-bodied globes still used by several companies today, each and every gas pump globe is highly collectible. Globes evolved from the early one-piece glass globes, to metal-band bodies with glass lenses, to glass bodies with removable lenses, to the plastic bodies formed in halves and sandwiched around lenses. Generally, the more graphic the globe, the more desirable it

is. Prices range from around $60 for plain plastic globes to over $15,000 for the most unique. Texaco globes are among the most popular, and, in fact, the highest price ever recorded for a globe was received for the cast Texaco Fire Chief Hat globe. Many reproductions are available, so be careful and know what you are buying. Globes were the primary subject of another Benjamin and Henderson book, *Gas Pump Globes*, published by Motorbooks International in 1994.

Cans

Motor-oil cans and other product containers first became popular among collectors in the late-1980s. Today, the common quart can—used from the early 1930s until the mid-1980s—is the most popular format, but five-quart cans and handy oilers are also very popular as well. As with signs and globes, the more graphic the can, the more desirable. Cans can be found in prices ranging from less than $5 for composite cans with plain graphics, to nearly $2,000 for the most graphically-appealing steel cans. Several reproductions are available, so, again, be careful and know what you are buying. No definitive work on cans has yet been completed.

Pumps

The first surge of interest in petroleum collectibles—back in the 1960s—was in gas pumps. Visible pumps were most desirable then, although in recent years visibles and pre-visibles have taken a backseat to ornate clock-face and other mechanically-intricate and decorative clock-face pumps. Mechanical calculating pumps, particularly with art-deco designs, are very popular as well. All pumps manufactured up until the "chrome" era of the 1960s are collectibles. Globes were the primary subject of another Benjamin and Henderson book, *Gas Pump Collectors Guide*, published by Motorbooks International in 1994.

Toys

The interest in toys is a relatively new phenomenon to petroleum-products collectors. Gasoline-related toys have been manufactured since the 1920s, and accurately-detailed, brand-specific toys have been offered since the 1930s. Some toys can be considered promotional items, while others were simply children's toys available to anyone.

Curved porcelain signs, like this one, were mounted on Texaco's visible and clock-face gas pumps. These curved pump signs date from the 1930s and early-1940s. *Dunbar's Gallery*

Texaco was the first company to regularly use promotional toys as part of its advertising, and it continues to do so today. Prices range from the current $20–range pricing for new toys to well over $1,000 for toys made as recently as 15 years ago.

Maps & Paper Items

Many collectors started their collections as children collecting road maps. Free road maps were perhaps the most widespread oil company promotion items of all time, with millions of maps having been given away from 1914 to the present. Most companies, Texaco included, abandoned the practice of producing and giving away maps in the 1970s, but all maps are considered collectible. Texaco maps are not as graphically appealing as those from some other brands, and, as a result, are not very valuable. While maps generally range in price from $1 to about $75, most Texaco maps fall into the $1–5 range.

Internal Corporate Items

Internal corporate items have recently found a place of interest with collectors. Employee pins

Texaco manufactured its own containers for many years, and this embossed lid was an example of the elaborate design used on some of its containers. *Richard Eaves Collection*

and badges, award items and trinkets—many of which fall into the "smalls" or "trinkets" category—are addressed in this book. Corporate publications are of interest as well, and price ranges depend on the type of item involved. Many items are hard to find, since they were never intended for use by the general public.

Trinkets
Advertising novelties are among the fastest growing items of all petroleum collectibles, in terms of interest. Salt and pepper shaker sets, oil-can banks, radios, and thousands more items are available. Virtually anything that ever had an oil com-

pany logo applied to it is collectible. Categories include items supplied by the oil companies themselves; items sanctioned by the oil companies for personalization by the local distributor or dealer; plus items supplied by advertising companies directly to distributors and dealers. Price ranges vary widely, and prices are rising.

Texaco "green cans" come in all shapes and sizes. Notice the unusual two-quart Texaco "Easy Pour" can and the decorative handy oilers from the 1920s and 1930s. *Marty Lineen*

Chapter 2

History of The Texas Company

1902–1910: The Texas Company

Oil exploration of the nineteenth century centered on the Pennsylvania oil region, an area that was roughly a diagonal oval on the map that extended from Erie and Cleveland south to Charleston, West Virginia. From this region came the world's best crude—ideal for refining and blending for lubrication. But by the beginning of the twentieth century, however, oil companies had begun exploration throughout the country, in Wyoming, California, Kansas, and along the Gulf Coast in Texas.

The wide open country of east Texas, outside Beaumont, came under close scrutiny of numerous oil hunters. Oil had been discovered

The most familiar gasoline image that was ever created, the classic Texaco logo has adorned stations, refineries, bulk plants, terminals and other Texaco facilities worldwide. In its most familiar incarnation, the logo appeared at some 40,000 Texaco stations in the form of the "banjo" sign, introduced in 1936. In later years, illuminated logos were seen atop banjo poles, and on building pylons such as the sign shown here in Clinton, South Carolina, 1989.

Old photographs of Texaco trucks, stations, and employees provide collectors a glimpse into the company's past. *Richard Eaves Collection*

at Corsicana, Texas, in the early 1890s, and some people believed that more would be found. Attention centered around an unusual rise in the otherwise flat country, a nob that came to be known as Spindletop.

Work had begun in 1899 at Spindletop, when geologist and driller Anthony Lucas became convinced that oil would be found under the dome. Financing for exploration came from a team of successful explorers from the Pennsylvania region, Jim Guffey and John Galey. With resources secured, Lucas' work began, and in January 1901 the modern era of the petroleum industry was born. Spindletop hill literally exploded with crude oil, as a gusher producing over 50,000 gallons a day blew out the derrick and opened the field for a mad rush of production. Out of the madness that followed, several companies that we are familiar with today were born, the most famous being the Guffey-Galey op-

With uncharacteristic snow hampering the operation in Decatur, Alabama, in 1918, a loyal Texaco tanker driver refills the tank serviced by this Texaco curb pump. An early etched and chimney capped globe advertises Texaco products in this image so typical of early petroleum marketing.

Automobile "garages" were among the first retailers of motor fuel and automotive supplies. Fitzhugh Auto Service in Cape Charles, Virginia, has been a Texaco dealer since 1907, and maintains a 1930s image intact, except for modern pumps still at curbside, in this 1987 photograph.

eration, known as Gulf Oil; and an oil storage and marketing firm based in Beaumont that incorporated in 1902 as The Texas Company.

Joseph Cullinan, already successful in the Corsicana fields, joined in and began operations in Beaumont, as the Texas Fuel Company, purchasing crude at over-production pricing and storing it at nearby Port Arthur. Cullinan, in conjunction with others, secured a drilling lease from the Guffey-Galey operation and began production as well. Refining operations began at Port Arthur in 1903, and sales offices for Texas Company-refined products were opened in many southern and eastern cities during the next several years. In 1906, the company adopted its cable address acronym "TEXACO" as its brand name, and true to its namesake state, in 1907, Texaco adopted a large red star, complete with a green "T," as its primary trademark.

From the beginning, Texaco was a marketer. Every conceivable product that could be made from oil was offered at an ever growing number of Texaco "sales offices." Today, Texaco's "sales office" concept seems strange for an oil company, and, perhaps, is best compared to the scattered offices of some suppliers of industrial commodities, such as W.W. Grainer (industrial supplies) or Prime Equipment (heavy equipment sales and rentals). In every city, town, or village Texaco ventured into, consumers welcomed the availability of oils, greases, kerosene, asphalt, roofing materials, and, of course, gasoline. The acceptance of the gasoline-powered automobile in the early years of this century demanded the development of a network of gasoline-sales outlets. Outside every Texaco sales office, a curb-side gasoline pump was installed. Stores that had Texaco kerosene accounts installed pumps and tanks, too, and soon Texaco gasoline was available throughout the company's marketing area.

1910–1925: Development of the Gas Station

With the introduction of the Ford Model T in 1908, the automobile was making great strides towards universal acceptance, and its pricing was coming within reach of the working man. To feed the new machine's appetite for petroleum products, every petroleum marketer of the day was selling gasoline in whatever manner possible. Among

Two scenes are shown of this unusual
Texaco dealer station in Mesa, Arizona, about 1950. Note the unusual
rooftop sign and the unexplained Conoco triangle sign mounted on the front of the canopy, and the fact that the
station office doubled as a barber shop. *Bob Mewes*

their accounts were grocery stores; drug stores; hardware stores; livery stables and blacksmith shops; a new innovation, the "automobile garage;" and even private residences where gasoline pumps could be installed at curbside. Texaco's Spindletop sibling, Gulf, pioneered the first off-street "filling station" in Pittsburgh in 1913, and within two years every major petroleum marketer had adopted the innovation and was operating "filling stations" of its own. Texaco's first off-street station opened in Brooklyn, New York, in 1914, and by the next year, Texaco's marketing expertise mandated the development of a common image to promote its products. Signage, gas pump globes, lubricants

Many Texaco stations in the Southeast included an integral canopy, proudly displaying Texaco lettering backlit by neon. This station was serving motorists on South Roan Street in Johnson City, Tennessee, in 1952. *Chip Flohe*

This most unusual Texaco station in Cashiers, North Carolina, has an additional sales area extending beyond the service bays. Perhaps this served as a souvenir shop in the beautiful mountain tourist town.

This Oak Ridge, Tennessee, Texaco station, photographed in 1969, shows one example of the Texaco "Matawan" station design. *Chip Flohe*

signs—all featured a unified appearance. Texaco was the first marketer to attempt to create such a consistent image for its stations, and it was the first marketer to identify its marketing facilities with a specific sign. Most locations where Texaco products were sold were existing Texaco sales offices. In the case of dealers operating the wide assortment of businesses mentioned above, the image was applied as best as possible.

Texaco began construction of showcase company-owned stations in major metropolitan areas, and was operating over 100 stations by 1920. These early company stations were marketing laboratories—sites where experimentation with marketing concepts could be carried out. From these experiments, it was determined that local agents—independent businessmen serving as "dealers"—stood the best chance of successfully serving the motoring public. Within a few years, Texaco products were sold in 43 states by independent dealers.

Dispensing equipment saw major refinements in this era, as well, with blind operation, stroke-measure pumps giving way to "visible" pumps in the early 1920s, and the visibles giving way to electrically operated clock-face pumps for high-speed fueling.

1925–1946: Coast To Coast—The Star That Shines All Night

Gasoline marketing in most areas was dominated by descendants of the Standard Oil Trust. Within its respective territories, Standard generally set the prevailing price, and with facilities in nearly

every town, it dominated the entire market. Competition was tough. Regional marketers that competed with Standard companies usually found themselves at a loss. Standard could reduce prices in specific markets to eliminate competition, yet maintain the necessary profit levels across the balance of its territory for an acceptable return. Anyone going head-to-head with a Standard company could not win. Texaco realized this, however, and chose to spread its operations so that it would never meet Standard head-on for any extended period of time. This philosophy located Texaco stations everywhere. It did not maintain market leadership in any one area, but instead settled for number two or number three positions everywhere. Averaged against Standard's dominance in restricted areas only, Texaco became the largest gasoline marketer in the world by the early 1930s.

Market solidification was accomplished with the 1928 purchase of California Petroleum (Calpet). After buying Calpet, Texaco converted its California stations and moved into the remaining four western states where it previously had no stations. In 1928, Texaco stations could be found in all 48 states—a statistic that it would maintain for over 50 years and would share with only one other oil company, Phillips Petroleum, in its nationwide surge in the 1960s.

Despite its high visibility, Texaco lubricants had only a mediocre acceptance in the marketplace. To properly merchandise its growing network of stations, the company needed a premium line of lubricants, which it acquired by purchasing Indian Refining in 1931. Sometime between 1915 and 1920, Indian Refining—which had been founded in the early 1900s in Lawrenceville, Illinois—had purchased New York City-based Havoline Oil Company. Havoline, founded in 1906, had been known for its superior lubricants, refined in a dewaxing method that removed paraffin deposits. Indian operated stations in 19 eastern states, but Texaco's interest was in the Havoline brand name and manufacturing process. Indian stations were quickly rebranded Texaco, but Havoline Oils would not bear the Texaco name until 1959. With its market expansion in the 1920s, Texaco opened stations in British Columbia and in metropolitan areas of other western Canada provinces. The expansion was moderately successful, but Texaco was

South Armistead Avenue in Hampton, Virginia, was "automobile row" when this photograph was taken in 1923. Texaco gasoline was being dispensed at curbside in front of the Chevrolet dealership.

looking to expand coast-to-coast in Canada, too. To accomplish this, it traded its western operations, known as Texaco Canada, to a leading Canadian marketer, McColl-Frontenac. McColl-Frontenac was itself a blend of lubricant manufacturers, McColl Brothers, founded in 1873, and Frontenac Refining, a gasoline refiner founded in 1925. Together, McColl-Frontenac operated stations across central and eastern Canada under the "Red Indian" brand. In return for its trade of Texaco Canada, Texaco acquired controlling interest in McColl-Frontenac. By 1940, Texaco brand names began replacing Red Indian product brand names, and following World War II, Texaco replaced the Red Indian brand altogether.

While Texaco was largely known as a domestic company, by 1930 it had a network of far-flung sales offices all over the world. It was a major marketer in Africa, Asia, and Australia, and maintained a marketing presence in Europe, as well, although it met with more competition there from local refiner-marketers. By the mid-1930s, however, Texaco could not properly supply its widespread marketing efforts, and was on the verge of pulling back from some areas, when a Standard company entered the picture.

Standard Oil Company of California, a domestic West Coast integrated oil company, had been exploring for oil in the Middle East when, in 1936, it discovered more than it could profitably

A single Fry visible pump, displaying a stained glass Texaco globe, was dispensing Texaco gasoline at this roadside garage outside Hampton, Virginia, in 1924.

transport back to the United States for refining and marketing. To make the most of the production, Standard Oil of California and Texaco formed a partnership combining Standard's production and Texaco's marketing. The new entity was named Arabian American Oil Company, and Texaco stations throughout the Eastern Hemisphere were rebranded Caltex. The operation and the brand survives today.

The 1930s saw the beginning of several Texaco elements that would become entrenched in the minds of the motoring public. First, Texaco branded its regular-grade gasoline "Fire Chief" in 1932, with much fanfare, including the company's first use of radio advertising on a national level, featuring comedian Ed Wynn as Texaco's "Fire Chief" spokesman. Second, in 1936, a Texaco station identification sign was developed for maximum recognition. The

familiar Texaco "banjo" sign—so called for its appearance—became the most familiar of any gasoline identification sign used this century. The visually appealing structure, with tapered pole, supporting yoke, and center-mounted sign, has long been a beacon to motorists in need of fuel, automotive repair, directions, or simply a place to stretch their legs.

A third element was the 1937 adoption of Walter Darwin Teague's classic Texaco station design. The gleaming white stations, with upper facade interrupted with three parallel green stripes topped by red stars and lettering, was the first "modern" station design adopted by any major oil company. With minor modifications alone, thousands would be built in the next 30 years.

Operation of select highway stations on a 24-hour basis was a fourth element that firmly implanted Texaco stations in the minds of motorists. Virtually every station of the era closed before midnight, which left all-night travelers without a source for fuel. Until 1939, when Texaco began a program that kept dealers operating stations all night; advertising for the program promoted "The Star That Shines All Night." And many a night the illuminated Texaco star has been a welcome beacon to motorists.

Texaco's premium grade gasoline, Sky Chief, was introduced in 1939 and became a fifth element responsible for ensuring Texaco's success. Sky Chief was the first modern premium that was not marketed simply as an ethylized version of a regular grade.

Finally, the 1938 introduction of the Registered Rest Room program that guaranteed cleanliness was, perhaps, more successful than anything else at altering the way Texaco filling stations were perceived by the public. Prior to this program's introduction, gas station rest rooms—where they existed at all—were usually ignored by dealers and abused by the motoring public. The cleanliness guarantee was a welcome reassurance to the traveling public.

As the era drew to a close, Texaco had grown to be a coast-to-coast marketer, weathered the Depression well, and had established an image that would carry it through almost to the present day. During the lean years of the War, Texaco supplied fuels and lubricants for the Allied efforts, and despite the loss of many dealers during the rationing years of the War, the company had a marketing structure in place to take advantage of the postwar boom.

1946–1960: Trust Your Car to the Man Who Wears the Star

The postwar era brought the peak of Texaco's marketing influence. The nationwide adaptation of the "Teague" Texaco stations made the familiar Texaco station an American icon. The image was repeated successfully at most of Texaco's 40,000 gasoline stations nationwide in the years between 1946 and 1950. Gasoline consumption—built upon the pent-up demand of the wartime era—was at an all-time high and no company was better positioned than Texaco to take advantage of the call of the open road. All Texaco had to do was

pump gas. In this era, however, Texaco began seeing itself as an institution, sponsoring the Metropolitan Opera and pioneering television broadcasts, including the ever popular "Texaco Star Theater" with Milton Berle. The oil refiner continued to entertain us for many years.

During this era, Texaco also continued to improve its products, introducing the additive Petrox to its formulas for the Sky Chief gasolines in 1954. We say formulas, plural, for in this era Texaco really began to promote its regional blending of fuels to meet specific climatic differences. Every refiner does this, but Texaco promoted it widely and made the motoring public aware of the need for different fuels for different conditions. In 1955, Texaco announced its first multigrade motor oil, Advanced Custom Made Havoline Special 10W30. While Esso and Phillips had pioneered multigrades several years before, Texaco's use of the widely accepted Havoline brand name probably furthered the market acceptance of multigrades more than any other factor.

The only significant marketing expansion in this era was the 1959 purchase of Long Island City, New York-based Paragon Refining. Paragon had been a gasoline marketer early on, but was primarily a supplier of heating oils to New York and New England—heating oil's strongest customer base. Texaco retained the use of the Paragon name for several years before phasing in the Texaco brand.

Texaco services were highly promoted, since the postwar era saw the final demise of the "filling station" and the overwhelming market share of the "service station." Automotive repair, sales of tires, batteries, and accessories, known as "TBA" in the industry, became a leading profit center for gasoline dealers nationwide. Texaco teamed with Firestone and B.F. Goodrich to supply much of the demand, and developed a line of automotive chemicals to meet the needs of the day. Motorists were encouraged by Texaco's televised spokesmen to "trust their car to the man who wears the star." And Americans did so nationwide in record numbers.

1960–1973: Interstates and New Images

What else is left to do once you've developed the perfect marketing image and have became a cultural icon, but to tinker with that image until you ruin it? Texaco began tinkering with its image

Complete automotive service, lubrication at an outside lift, curbside air, and Texaco gasoline and motor oils were offered at this Phoebus, Virginia, Texaco station in 1927. A modern Texaco station, still offering repairs and full service, sits opposite this site today.

in about 1960, modifying the famous "Teague" Texaco image in an attempt to modernize it. New station designs were adopted, with the first re-designs being modifications of the existing image. In 1962, experimentation began with a hexagonal Texaco logo, although most of the public wouldn't see the replacement for the classic, circular logo until 1967. Admittedly, some adaptation was nec-essary, since the market was changing. Beginning in 1956, the federal government began construc-tion of the Interstate Highway System, replacing many miles of the older two lane roads with multi-lane highways with controlled access. No services were allowed directly on the new interstates, and gasoline marketers vied for choice positions at in-

terchanges. Texaco built thousands of stations along the new highways, and many once-prosper-ous sites on formerly busy highways, now bypassed, died a slow and painful death.

In response to the first government effort to beautify the American roadside, all gasoline mar-keters began experimentation with station designs to replace their gleaming porcelain designs with more refined structures. In 1964, Texaco intro-duced the "Matawan" station, featuring natural rock facings, expanses of glass, and service bays turned away from traffic. The image worked, and many locations with high visibility were rebuilt. Dominant colors were greens, golds, oranges, and blacks. Unfortunately, the existing porcelain

Can anyone believe that Texaco is still trying to improve on this image? Photographed at Mebane, North Carolina, in 1957. *James Covington*

Teague stations that were re-imaged to match the Matawan stations were often hideous. Black letters and stripes of gold facades, trimmed with orange and green accents, did little to beautify the cultural icons. The new station appearance was not universally accepted, though, as many Texaco distributors opted to maintain their classic Teague images. With an independent jobber network, and little central control, many Teague stations identified with banjo signs remained so until the next re-imaging in the 1980s, and indeed a few even survive today.

1973–1980: The Shortage Years

Survival was the name of the game in the 1970s, as the 1973 oil shortage and the later short-age in 1978 saw many gasoline marketers "circle the wagons" and retreat from far-flung markets. Texaco's competitor for nationwide marketing, Phillips—which had completed its coast-to-coast marketing in 1967 with the purchase and conversion of Tidewater Associated Flying A stations on the West Coast and in Hawaii, and the establishment of a single station in Anchorage, Alaska—went at its territory with an ax, eliminating marketing in the far west, the northeast, and everywhere else that it was not profitable. But Texaco stood its ground. Holding its head high, the company maintained its 50-state marketing philosophy during the shortages, although thousands of individual dealers were lost. Also in this era, Texaco began its first serious experimentation with "split-

Texaco purchased and rebranded the Calpet stations in California in 1927. This location was offering a motor-grade gasoline still branded "Calpet" when photographed here in 1936. *Ron Johnson*

island," full-service/self-service stations, with gas-only self-service pumpers, and with a new marketing concept pioneered in Minneapolis—the gasoline convenience store. Texaco distributors and dealers were slower than most to innovate, however, and most of Texaco's marketing network remained the same throughout the shortage years. By 1980, however, profitability became an issue, and at long last some areas of the country were abandoned. Texaco closed distribution facilities in the Northern Plains—Montana, North Dakota, Kansas, Minnesota, Wisconsin, and Iowa—and in the highly-competitive, industrialized areas of Ohio, Indiana, and much of Illinois. Even today, it is not unusual to see a relatively intact Teague Texaco station, less the sign in front and those six letters over the sales office, selling un-branded gasoline in these areas. Texaco sold stations to operating dealers, some were almost given away, and re-

moved its imaging. Many such stations continue to operate today. Much of the Midwest marketing was sold to Sinclair, and to this day, it is not at all uncommon to see Sinclair dealer stations with stars on one end of the building.

1980–1990: Hard Times

Positioning itself for profitability by abandoning parts of its market, Texaco's next move was to become more self-sufficient in crude oil production. It greatly expanded its own exploration efforts in areas where it would be less vulnerable to OPEC influences that had created the gasoline shortages of the 1970s. And it went shopping for a crude-oil producer, as well.

By 1983, Texaco had pinpointed Getty Oil, J. Paul Getty's firm that had worldwide crude production, proven reserves, and only a minimal market presence to support in the Northeastern Getty (formerly Flying A) stations and the Midwestern Skelly stations (Getty had controlled Skelly for years). Getty, however, had already begun merger negotiations with Pennzoil, which was attempting a merger for much the same reasoning as Texaco. Pennzoil and Getty signed a merger agreement in January 1984, but within two days, Texaco announced it had purchased control of Getty on the open market. Pennzoil cried foul, and a series of lawsuits for interfering with an on-going merger culminated in a 1988 settlement that forced Texaco to the brink of bankruptcy, having to pay Pennzoil in excess of $3 billion.

Despite the poor judgment (or poor timing), Texaco had been the successful bidder and now controlled Getty. As the new owner, Texaco shortly sold off Getty's Northeastern operations, which continue to operate today. The Getty Midwestern Skelly operations in most areas were re-branded as Texaco stations. Better positioned with the Skelly assets, Texaco signs were again seen in Kansas, Minnesota, and Iowa.

Also during the 1980s, Texaco introduced a new logo and image, returning to its traditional roots. Stations were decorated in gray and black with red accents, and a circular sign (on a black field) was adopted, with a red circular area and "T," and a white star. This time, the re-imaging was not as "voluntary," either: Most Texaco stations got a complete make-over in the 1980s; those stations that did not adopt the new look were eliminated, left un-branded and without access to Texaco's credit card network.

1990–Present: Star of the American Road

Following the merger-mania of the 1980s, Texaco's refining and marketing operations were spun off from the rest of the company, and the Texaco you see today is actually several companies. Star Enterprise is the Saudi Arabian-controlled refining and marketing division that supplies gasoline throughout the south and east. Texaco Refining and Marketing serves the same function in the west. Texaco Lubricants Company supplies the Havoline and Ursa motor oils sold by Texaco stations and many other retailers nationwide. The divisions were created to maximize profits, and today's Texaco, as a whole, is stronger than ever.

Open-air service bays were typical of service station arrangement in balmy California. This station was photographed in Southern California in 1936. *Ron Johnson*

Today, Texaco—through Texaco Refining and Marketing—operates over 4,000 stations in over 20 states. Star Enterprise operates nearly 10,000 stations in over 25 states. In 1996, Texaco/Star Enterprise was a primary sponsor of the summer Olympics, and, in conjunction with the event, introduced a new image package at an Atlanta area station. Having blended the Skelly truck stop network into its own, Texaco now operates more branded truck stops than any other marketer. Havoline motor oils—from Texaco Lubricants Company-—enjoys widespread acceptance in the marketplace, and Texaco has been a major sponsor in NASCAR sporting events, having backed the late Davey Allison and his successor, Ernie Irvan. Best of all for petroleum-memorabilia collectors, Texaco has become much more aware of its own history and is cooperating with collectors in an attempt to preserve Texaco memorabilia and is sanctioning the re-creation of a Teague Texaco station in the Henry Ford Museum in Dearborn, Michigan.

As Texaco approaches its 100th anniversary, in 2002, we are sure to see more interest in the company's history among Texaco employees, jobbers, and dealers, as well as the story of the twentieth century oil industry that will be told through the surviving artifacts.

Chapter 3

Texaco Station Design

Texaco was one of the first companies to construct its stations based on a standard design. By standardizing its stations, two ends were accomplished: First, construction costs were controlled by economies of scale—savings were realized by buying huge quantities of building materials, and installation crews worked faster when repeating the design; second, the consistent image created instant brand-recognition, since a Texaco station in Newport News would look just like one in Salt Lake City. Motorists would equate the quality products and friendly service of their neighborhood Texaco station with others nationwide.

Through the years, the design of Texaco's stations has changed periodically, reflecting the styles and values of the times. This chapter examines several of the more familiar Texaco station designs that generations of Americans have come to recognize.

Texaco stations have changed dramatically through the years. These photos illustrae the various station tyles. Richard Eaves Collection

Gloucester Court House, Virginia, has been home to Edgehill Texaco since 1916. At this "Denver" style station, the "Texaco 2000" image competes with a stained glass Texaco sign from the 1920s. Still in operation, this station was photographed here in 1984.

Texaco Denver Station Circa 1921

Texaco's earliest attempt at station design resulted in beautiful stations that looked like gingerbread houses. Each station had a sharply-peaked, tile roof and projecting towers at the front corners of the buildings that were topped with glass balls and which served as canopy columns. These stations used the stained glass Texaco window in the canopy portico, and it was internally illuminated for nighttime recognition.

Texaco Type "EM" Station (The "Teague" Texaco) Circa 1937

The "EM" or "Teague" design is the classic Texaco station, an American icon and the most repeated commercial building design of the twentieth century. Presented by industrial designer Walter Darwin Teague to Texaco in 1937, the "EM" was widely accepted because it could be used for new locations, as well as retrofit onto existing stations. The design called for white porcelain building panels to be used, but white stucco or white

This 1955 photograph showcases a Knoxville, Tennessee, Texaco station that includes all of the visual elements that make the "Teague" station design so attractive. Note the Banjo sign. *Chip Flohe*

Texaco Type "EP" Station Circa 1960

In the early 1960s, Texaco began experimentation with modifications to the Teague design. One of the most frequently seen adaptations involved repositioning the green stripe panels to the top projecting edge of the building, with service bay areas higher than the adjacent office. Lettering appeared on top of the sales office area, with stars or the motto "Service You Can Trust" above the bays. Another variation of this design included a projecting pylon with a large internally-illuminated Texaco logo displayed on all visible sides.

Texaco Matawan Station Circa 1964

In response to other oil companies experimenting with more appealing designs for their stations, Texaco designers introduced the Matawan station in 1964. The station was built on several designs, but primarily used rock walls for solid areas of the station structure with open, glass areas broken up

The "Teague" Texaco design was so versatile in that it could be constructed with any number of service bays; most examples, such as this Memphis location, had just two bays. Stations with anywhere from no bays to five are known to exist. *Chip Flohe*

painted brick was acceptable. The facade was broken up by three parallel green stripes, with red stars spaced above service bays and red "TEXACO" lettering above the sales office. Green lettering below the stripes identified the dealer and services offered. Thousands of these stations were built or adapted, with any number of service bays and even a few without bays. Portable trailers that resembled the Teague design were used as offices during rebuilds, but few have survived intact.

By the 1960s, Texaco considered its image somewhat dated, so it began experimenting with updated designs. This 1960 Texaco station in Kingsport, Tennessee, was one of the last to be constructed in the conventional design. *Chip Flohe*

Texaco stations competing for attention amid a crowded development strip used this offset-pole projecting Texaco sign to stand out from other signs along the roadside. *Chip Flohe*

by brightly colored panels for partitions or curtain walls. Service bay entrances were usually at the side, but some adaptations of this design called for front entrances. Few of these stations remain today, and fewer still remain intact, but the Matawan was testament to a Texaco in transition.

Texaco 2000 Station Circa 1983

With the adoption of the Texaco 2000 image standards in 1982, a new station design was born. Buildings were painted gray, with black fascia bands offset by red molding along the bottom. Canopy fascias were solid black, with red lettering and the new red, circular logo and white star-design signage. Most designs were for convenience stores, but some service stations were adapted to

this design. Most Texaco stations, today, are of the Texaco 2000 design.

Texaco Star Mart Circa 1996

In the spring of 1996, in conjunction with the Texaco sponsorship of the 1996 Summer

Hexagon signage, on an offset pole no less, and modern pumps are the only indication that this Joanna, South Carolina, Texaco station was photographed in 1989, rather than 1959.

Several variations of the Texaco type "EP" station were constructed. This version, photographed near Oak Ridge, Tennessee, in 1967, includes an attached canopy with rooftop signage. *Chip Flohe*

Olympics in Atlanta, Georgia, and as part of an effort to create a "global" image in today's marketplace, Texaco introduced a significant modification to the Texaco 2000 design. Buildings remained gray, but now featured red fascia bands and gray wrap-around corners, not unlike BP station designs. Texaco marketers subscribing to Texaco's "Star-Mart" convenience store format were offered a special "Star-Mart" image for the building. The canopy was the primary focus of change, though, with sweeping round corners and a red neon bottom band offsetting the gloss-black fascia. Texaco lettering remained red, but was recessed into the fascia. The Texaco logo was also recessed, domed like a globe lens, and accented by a comet-like tail. Rounded columns and enhanced pump graphics—each featuring rounder, smoother designs—completed the package. As of this writing, several marketers are building or remodeling stations to match the new image.

One of the most spectacular station designs of the early 1960s was this version of the Texaco "EP," complete with illuminated sign in pylon tower, as seen here at Clinton, South Carolina, in 1989.

Olive green, harvest gold, and orange accents are typical of colors used on Texaco "Matawan" stations of the 1970s. This station was found intact at Lincoln Park, Colorado, in 1990.

This hybrid design incorporates the Texaco stained glass window sign into the Teague design in this 1940 prototype. Very few of these stations were ever constructed, and we know of none surviving. This station stood in Rochester, New York.

This Texaco truck stop on U.S. 29 just north of Danville, Virginia, is the utmost in modern convenience. Five automotive fueling islands and multiple truck islands in the rear serve motorists who've been beckoned in by the new global Texaco "Star Mart" imaging. Constructed in 1996 by Petroleum Pump and Tank Company, this writer's employer, for W. Henry Hardy, Inc. of Danville, who has distributed Texaco products since 1921.

Chapter 4

Texaco Globes

The Texas Company

Texaco globes are among the most popular Texaco items to Texaco collectors, and they are also among the most popular globes for globe collectors. All but the most unusual Texaco globes are readily available, although the more unusual ones bring prices relative to their popularity.

Note: Reference to the "TEXACO logo" refers to the "classic" red star and green "T" emblem with black "TEXACO" across the upper portion of the star.

Texaco Gasoline/Motor Oil (chimney cap)
1915–1917 (5)   OPE   no listing
The first Texaco globe, introduced with the emphasis placed on "image" in 1915. Red areas are etched into a milk glass body. Red globe face with white Texaco logo, red star and green "T" in center. White "TEXACO" arched around top, "GASOLINE" around bottom, with white "MOTOR" left of logo's center, "OIL &" to right of logo's center on red band.

Texaco (chimney cap)
1917–1920 (5)   OPE $2,500–3,500
One-piece etched, chimney-capped globe with Texaco logo on globe face.

Later one-piece Texaco globes had the design cast as part of the globe, resulting in raised details in the logo. This beautiful example of a Texaco "cast" globe displays its original baked-on paint very well. *Petroleum Collectibles Monthly*

Companion to the one-piece cast Texaco globe is this one-piece cast "raised letter" Texaco Ethyl globe. Texaco Ethyl was introduced in 1926. *Petroleum Collectibles Monthly*

Texaco early wide body
1917–1920 (5)   OPE $2,500–3,000
One-piece etched globe with Texaco logo on globe face.

Texaco leaded glass globe
1918–1925 (5)   22" inserts   no listing

Texaco leaded glass globe
1918–1925 (4)   13.75" Inserts $3,500–4,500
Most unusual gas pump globes of all times. Metal bodies with lead channel framework for stained glass (colors) and milk glass (white area) lenses in the image of the Texaco logo.

Texaco marketing throughout the Eastern Hemisphere, where Texaco operated in partnership with Standard Oil of California, was carried out under the Caltex brand, and gas pumps in Africa and Asia were identified by this globe.

Texaco
1920–1926 (4)   OPE $1,700–2,400

Texaco
1924–1932 (6)   OPB   no listing

Texaco
1926–1932 (3)   OPC $900–1,400
One-piece globe with Texaco logo. Design may be etched into the globe, a baked-enamel finish on the surface of the globe, or baked enamel on a cast, raised feature image, as noted above.

Texaco Ethyl
1926–1930 (4)   OPC $1,600–2,200
One-piece raised-letter globe with black "TEX-ACO" above center Texaco logo and black "ETHYL" below.

Texaco Ethyl
1930–1932 (5)   OPC   no listing
One piece raised-letter globe with red outer border and white "TEXACO" above center Texaco logo and white "ETHYL" below.

Texaco Aviation
1920s   (6)   OPC   no listing
One piece raised-letter globe. Black outline ring around edge of face. Black-outlined Texaco logo in center with red "propeller" blade to either side of logo. Black "AVIATION" arched around top, "GASOLINE" around bottom. So far, only one example is known to exist.

Texaco etched milk glass lens
1927–1932 (5)   15" metal $2,500–3,200
White, etched milk glass globe lens with black-outlined Texaco logo in center. Wide white outer band surrounds logo outline.

Texaco
1927–1932 (6)   16.5" metal   no listing

Texaco
1927–1932 (4)   15" metal $1,800–2,400
White globe lens with black-outlined Texaco logo in center. Wide white outer band surrounds logo outline.

Texaco Ethyl
1927–1930 (5)   15" metal   no listing
White globe lens with black-outlined Texaco logo in center. Wide white outer band surrounds logo outline. Black "TEXACO" arched around top, "ETHYL" around bottom.

Texaco Ethyl
1930–1932 (6)   15" metal   unconfirmed
White globe lens with black-outlined Texaco logo in center. Wide red outer band surrounds logo outline. White "TEXACO" arched around top, "ETHYL" around bottom.

Texaco Ethyl
1930–1932 (6)   18" neon   no listing
White globe lens with black-outlined Texaco logo in center. Wide red outer band surrounds logo outline. White "TEXACO" arched around top, "ETHYL" around bottom. Large lens in a special body outfitted with a neon tube ring around the inside of the band for illumination.

One of the more desirable Texaco globes available to collectors today is the Texaco Ethyl. The red border is reminiscant of Texaco signage from the era, and this globe immediately predates the Texaco Sky Chief globe. Texaco Sky Chief replaced Texaco Ethyl in late 1938.

Sky Chief was introduced in 1939 as Texaco's premium grade motor fuel. Shown here is a postwar Texaco Sky Chief globe. Note the white border "T," on a plastic "Capcolite" body. *Petroleum Collectibles Monthly*

Texaco Fire Chief hat
1932   (5)   cast shape   no listing
Beautifully detailed cast globe in the shape of a fireman's hat on a white stand. Red-painted hat with black highlights. Black-outlined Texaco logo in front shield of hat. Red "FIRE-CHIEF" on white base area. Less than five examples are known to exist, and recent sales have taken this globe to record prices for all globes.

Texaco Fire Chief
1932–1935   (6)   13.5" glass   no listing
The rarest Texaco globe, with no examples known at this time. It has been confirmed to exist by appearance in old photos. Black-outlined white globe face with detailed red/white/black/gold fireman's hat in center. Black-outlined Texaco logo at upper left of hat, with red "FIRE-CHIEF" across bottom of globe face.

Texaco Fire Chief
1932–1940   (6)   36B baked top $800–1,200
White cast top for Tokehim Model 36 and 36B gas pumps. Baked finish, black-outlined red "FIRE CHIEF" across both sides of casting.

Texaco porcelain sign globe
1930–1940   (5)   special $1,500–2,000
A specially-made porcelain globe designed for external spotlight illumination, used on pumps that were not designed for an internally illuminated globe, and for use in those areas that did not yet have electric power. Black-outlined white Texaco with red star and black-outlined green "T." Standard size, black base.

Texaco (black border "T")
1935–1944   (3)   13.5" glass $300–400

Texaco (black border "T")
1935–1944   (4)   Gill $300–400
White globe face with black outline ring. Large red star in center, with black-outlined green "T" in center of star. Black "TEXACO" across upper star, with black "Reg. T.M." below star. Most originals are dated.

Texaco Ethyl
1932–1939   (4)   13.5" glass $1,000–1,500
Red globe face with black-outlined Texaco logo in center. White "TEXACO" arched around top, "ETHYL" around bottom of red outer band.

Texaco Sky Chief (black border "T")
1939–1944   (4)   13.5" glass $325–425

Texaco Sky Chief (black border "T")
1939–1944   (5)   Gill $350–450
Green globe face with black band across bottom and black-outlined white band and series of green and white stripes across top. Black-outlined red "wing" logo with Texaco logo in center covers most of sign face. Red "SKY CHIEF" across upper white band.

Texaco (white border "T")
1944–1968   (2)   13.5" glass $300–375

Texaco (white border "T")
1944–1968   (3)   Gill $325–400

Texaco (white border "T")
1944–1968   (2)   CAPCO $225–275
White globe face with black outline ring. Large red star in center, with white-outlined green "T" in center of star. Black "TEXACO" across upper star, with black "Reg. T.M." below star. Most originals are dated.

Texaco Sky Chief (white border "T")
1944–1968 (2)   13.5" glass $300–375
Texaco Sky Chief (white border "T")
1944–1968 (3)   Gill $325–400

Texaco Sky Chief (white border "T")
1944–1968 (2)   CAPCO $225–275
Green globe face with black band across bottom and black-outlined white band and series of green and white stripes across top. Black-outlined red "wing" logo with Texaco logo in center covers most of sign face. Red "SKY CHIEF" across upper white band.

Indian Gas
1932–1946 (4)   13.5" glass $475–650
White globe face with large red dot in center. Blue "INDIAN" arched around top, "GAS" around bottom.

Texaco Diesel Chief
1939–1944 (5)   13.5" glass   no listing
White globe face with red lower half. Red injector nozzle projecting into upper white area with thick red lines forming spray image covering white area. Large Texaco logo superimposed over spray at top. Black "DIESEL/CHIEF" on lower red area. An extremely rare globe that was modified at the end of World War II, because of its similarity in appearance to the Japanese rising sun image.

Texaco Diesel Chief
1944–1968 (4)   Gill $500–850

Texaco Diesel Chief
1944–1968 (5)   13.5" glass $500–850

Texaco Diesel Chief
1944–1968 (4)   CAPCO $400–650
White globe face with red lower half. Red injector nozzle projecting into upper white area with thin red lines forming spray image covering white area. Large Texaco logo superimposed over spray at top. White "DIESEL/CHIEF" on lower red area.

Texaco Diesel Fuel
1944–1968 (5)   Gill $550–900

Texaco Diesel Fuel
1944–1968 (4)   CAPCO $450–700

Rare and highly desirable, any Texaco Ethyl globe has seen a great increase in interest, and value, in recent years. The metal framed globes found on the West Coast are among the most unusual.

White globe face with green lower half. Green injector nozzle projecting into upper white area with thin green lines forming spray image covering white area. Large Texaco logo superimposed over spray at top. White "DIESEL/FUEL" on lower green area.

Indian Oil & Refining Co.,
Lawrenceville, Illinois
Indian Refining Company was a refiner and marketer with branded gasoline stations in 19 Northeast and North Central states. It is best remembered for the motor oil brand Havoline, introduced in 1906 by Havoline Oil Company of New York, which Indian Refining purchased in the later years of this century's second decade. Texaco continues to use the Havoline brand today. Texaco purchased Indian in 1931 in order to acquire the Havoline process patents.

Indian Gasoline "It Also..."
1910–1915 (6)   12" metal   no listing
Extremely early globe. White globe face with red "INDIAN/GASOLINE" across top. Black slogan "IT ALSO MAKES A DIFFERENCE" across bottom of face.

Indian gasoline was marketing in eastern and north-central states prior to 1931, when Texaco purchased Indian in order to secure manufacturing procedures for waxfree motor oil. The Indian trademark "Havoline" survives today, and Indian Gas survived as a trademark for Texaco's motor grade gasoline until after World War II. This rare and beautiful globe dates from the late-1910s.

Indian w/running Indian
1915–1924 (4) OPE $4,500–6500
Etched milk glass globe with detailed brown and black running Indian in center. Blue "INDIAN" arched around top, "GASOLINE" around bottom. Blue "Havoline" etched down each side of globe.

Indian w/running Indian
1915–1924 (5) OPE 4" base no listing
Similar to the globe listed above with a different body style and a 4" diameter base. Etched milk glass globe with detailed brown and black running Indian in center. Blue "INDIAN" arched around top, "GASOLINE" around bottom. Blue "Havoline" etched down each side of globe.

Indian w/running Indian
1915–1924 (4) 15" metal $3,000–5,000
White globe face with detailed brown and black running Indian in center. Blue "INDIAN" arched

around top, "GASOLINE" around bottom.

Indian Hi Test
1915–1924 (5) OPE $1,800–2,600
Etched globe with white globe face. Large red dot in center with white lightning bolt across dot. Blue "INDIAN" arched around top, "HI-TEST" around bottom. Blue "Havoline" etched down each side of globe.

Indian (red dot around Indian)
1922–1925 (5) OPE no listing
Transitional image globe. Etched globe with white globe face. Large red dot in center with running Indian on dot. Blue "INDIAN" arched around top, "GASOLINE" around bottom. Blue "HAVO-LINE" vertical down side of globe body.

Indian Red Ball Gasoline
1922–1925 (6) OPE no listing
Etched globe with white globe face. Large red dot in center. Blue "INDIAN" arched around top, "GASOLINE" around bottom, "RED" to left of center dot, "BALL" to right. Blue "HAVOLINE" vertical down side of globe body.

Indian Gas (milk glass face)
1924–1926 (5) 15" metal no listing
Etched milk glass globe face. Large red dot in center of globe face. Blue "INDIAN" arched around top, "GAS" around bottom.

Indian Gas "Havoline"
1924–1934 (4) OPE $1,800–2,400
Etched globe with white globe face. Large red dot in center of globe face. Blue "INDIAN" arched around top, "GAS" around bottom with blue "HAVOLINE" vertical down side of globe body.

Indian Gas "Havoline"
1924–1934 (5) OPB $1,600–2,200
Baked-finish globe with white globe face. Large red dot in center of globe face. Blue "INDIAN" arched around top, "GAS" around bottom with blue "HAVOLINE" vertical down side of globe body.

Indian Gas
1924–1934 (4) OPB $1,200–1,800
Baked finish globe with white globe face. Large red dot in center of globe face. Blue "INDIAN"

arched around top, "GAS" around bottom.

Indian Gas
1932 (5) 15" metal $1,000–1,600
White globe face with large red dot in center of globe face. Blue "INDIAN" arched around top, "GAS" around bottom. Probably dates from after Texaco purchased Indian Refining and the brand name "Indian" became Texaco's motor-grade fuel. Metal-band Texaco globes are found on the West Coast, where Texaco purchased several marketing firms in the 1927–28 era.

California Petroleum Company
California Petroleum Company was a west coast refining and marketing operation that Texaco purchased in 1928. The expansion into five far-western states in that year made Texaco the first gasoline brand to be offered in all 48 states.

Calpet Gas
1920–1927 (5) 15" metal $300–600
White globe face with large, rounded-corner diamond design covering most of globe face. Solid band across center of diamond, with white "CALPET" in band. Smaller, white "GASOLINE" below band.

Paragon Oil Company, Long Island City, New York
Paragon was primarily a fuel oil marketer, operating in the metropolitan New York market and throughout Long Island. Texaco purchased Paragon in 1958, and continued to use its brand name until about 1964, when all Paragon facilities were rebranded Texaco.

Note: No globes known. Existing Paragon globes are from a Toledo-based independent.

McColl-Frontenac Oil Company, Ltd., Toronto, Ontario, Canada
McColl Brothers, Ltd. - Toronto, Ontario
McColl Brothers was established in 1873 as a manufacturer of industrial lubricants. It expanded into gasoline marketing in 1916, primarily as a distributor, and in 1925 began operating a refinery for the production of its new gasoline, branded "Red Indian."

Some Indian stations used this metal band globe as an alternate to the one piece examples in the late-1910s and early-1920s.

Note: No globes are known with the Red Indian brand name dated prior to the McColl-Frontenac merger.

Frontenac Oil Refineries, Ltd. - Montreal, Quebec
Established in October 1925, Frontenac was basically a reorganization of the earlier entity, Nations Oil Refineries, Ltd. The company introduced its Frontenac brand name shortly after the company was organized, and it remained the primary brand name used by Frontenac until 1932 when the McColl "Red Indian" brand was adopted.

Frontenac Gas
1926–1932 (5) OPB $600–1200
White globe with baked-on finish. Large, black-outlined red "FRONTENAC" in bowtie lettering across center of globe face with black-outlined red "GAS" below. Black-outlined red "double arrow" design at top of globe.

Frontenac Gas
1920s (6) 15" metal unconfirmed
Description not available.

Later one-piece Indian Gas globes carried the more familiar "red dot" trademark and the motor oil brand name "Havoline" on the side.

Frontenac Gas
1930–1932   (5)   13.5" glass $250–400
White globe face with large black-outlined red "FRONTENAC" in bowtie lettering across center of globe face with black-outlined red "GAS" below. Black-outlined red "double arrow" design at top of globe.

Nations Oil Refineries, Ltd. - Montreal, Quebec
Nations Oil Refineries, Ltd., was a refining and marketing company purchased by Frontenac Oil Refineries, Ltd., in the 1926 establishment of the company. They had operated under the Cyclo brand name for several years, but the Frontenac brand name soon replaced Cyclo.

Cyclo Gas No-Knock Motor Fuel
1925–1930 (5)   OPB $800–1,200
White glass globe with baked finish. Black outline ring with green center circle. Black-outlined red "NO-KNOCK" arched around top, "MOTOR FUEL" around bottom, with black-outlined red "Cyclo/Gas" in center green circle.

Cyclo
              (6)   13.5" glass   unconfirmed
Description not available.

Cyclo Ethy
              (5)   13.5" glass $650–750
Black outline around white outer band and around green center circle. Black-outlined red "NO-KNOCK" arched around top, "MORE POWER" around bottom in outer ring. Black-outlined red "CYCLO/ETHYL" in center circle.

McColl-Frontenac Oil Company, Ltd.
After the merger of McColl Bros. and Frontenac Oil Company in November 1927, the two entities continued to operate separately until 1932, when the operations were completely merged. The merged entity continued to market under the "Marathon" brand name, using the red Indian logo. The brand name later became representative of the "Red Indian" logo. In the late 1930s, Texaco began investing in McColl-Frontenac, and in return, in 1939, McColl-Frontenac purchased Texaco's operations that had been established in Western Canada. The unique name and image continued to be used through the gradual phasing-in of Texaco brand names, which began in 1941. The final Red Indian signs came down in 1947. Increased investment by Texaco led to the corporate name change in 1959, when McColl-Frontenac became Texaco Canada, Ltd. Operations continued under the Texaco corporate name and brand names until 1990, when Imperial Oil, the Canadian Exxon affiliate, purchased Texaco Canada. The Esso brand name replaced Texaco at hundreds of stations nationwide, although Texaco lubricants continue to be available for the automotive aftermarket.

Marathon Hi Test Gasoline
1932–1935 (5)   OPB $1,800–2,500
White globe face with large red Indian head with
black details in center of globe face. Black
"MARATHON" arched around top, blue "BLUE"
around bottom with black "ANTI-" left of Indian
head and "KNOCK" to right. All known examples
were repainted by the company in the 1930s.

Marathon Blue
1932–1935 (5)   OPB $1,800–2,500
White globe face with large red Indian head with
black details in center of globe face. Black
"MARATHON" arched around top, blue
"BLUE" around bottom with black "ANTI-" left
of Indian head and "KNOCK" to right. All
known examples were repainted by the company
in the 1930s.

*Note: many one piece marathon globes have painted
finishes only.*
Marathon Gasoline
1932–1935 (5)   13.5" glass   no listing
White globe face with large red Indian head with
black details in center of globe face. Black
"MARATHON" arched around top, "GASO-
LINE" below.

Marathon Blue
1932–1935 (5)   13.5" glass $1,500–2,500
White globe face with large red Indian head with
black details in center of globe face. Black
"MARATHON" arched around top, blue "BLUE"
around bottom with black "ANTI-" left of Indian
head and "KNOCK" to right.

Red Indian
1935–1947 (4)   13.5" glass $1,400–2,000
White globe face with large red Indian head with
black details in center of globe face. Black "RED"
arched around top, "INDIAN" below.

Regent Refining, Ltd. - Port Credit, Ontario
Regent was an Ontario based refiner-marketer that
McColl-Frontenac purchased in 1957. Stations
were rebranded Texaco.

Regent
1946–1957 (4)   13.5" glass $400–600

Texaco regular grade diesel
fuel pumps were identified by this globe. The design
resembles the porcelain pump sign used in the same
era. *Petroleum Collectibles Monthly*

Blue globe face with white circular band around red
dot in center. White band horizontal across center
of globe face. Blue "REGENT" on center band.

Caltex: Arabian-American Oil Company, New York, New York

In 1936 Standard Oil Company of California
(Socal) entered into a joint venture with The
Texas Company to market petroleum products in
the Eastern Hemisphere under the Caltex brand.
Prior to this time, Texaco had established markets
in Europe, Asia, Africa, and Australia. Crude
poor, Texaco found it difficult to supply refined products
for its far-flung marketing. When Socal discovered
crude in abundant quantities on the Arabian
Peninsula, it offered Texaco the opportunity to
market its products. Jointly, Texaco and Socal
formed the Arabian American Oil Company, and
the "Caltex" brand was selected as the marketing
name for the new joint venture. In 1967, the part-
ners went their separate ways in Europe, but
throughout the remaining Eastern Hemisphere
Caltex signs still appear over hundreds of gasoline

stations, many of them designed far differently than the convenience stores that we in the United States have become accustomed to. Despite markings reading "Registered U.S. Patent Office" on some items, the Caltex brand has *never* been used, except, perhaps, for some obscure marketing experiment, in the United States or Canada.

Caltex
1936–1950 (4)   OPC $1,200–1,800
One-piece cast globe with raised details. Black outline with red star in center. Black "CALTEX" across center of star.
Caltex
1940–1970 (4)   CAPCO $300–500
White globe face with black outline around red star in center. Black "CALTEX" across center of star.

Other Foreign

Texaco star (Asian)
1930–1936 (5)   cast star
$3,500–5,000
Milk glass globe cast in the shape of a three-dimensional star. Black-outlined green "T" in center, with black "TEXACO" across the bottom. Used in Eastern Asian and Australian markets prior to the formation of Arabian-American Oil Company by Texaco and Socal.

Texaco hexagon (European)
1967–1970 (5)   one-piece plastic
$300–500
White plastic halves assembled back-to-back. Red border, elongated hexagon logo with Texaco "red star" logo at bottom of red band. Black "TEXACO" across center of white area of hexagon.

Texaco Marcas Registras (Cuban)
1930s   (5)   13.5" glass
$300–500
Black-outlined white globe face with large, red star in center. Black-outlined green "T" in center of star with black "TEXACO" across upper area of star. This Cuban/Caribbean version has "Marcas Registras" across bottom below star.

Texaco premium grade "Diesel Chief" diesel fuel pumps were identified by this globe. The design resembles the porcelain pump sign used in the same era. *Petroleum Collectibles Monthly*

The cast Fire Chief hat is perhaps the rarest Texaco globe. Less than five examples are known to exist. *Petroleum collectibles Monthly*

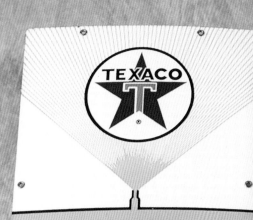

FUEL CHIEF 1
(DIESEL FUEL)

FIRE-CHIEF
GASOLINE

TEXACO
REG. T.M.

Marine White

Clean,
Clear,
GOLDEN

TEXACO
MOTOR OIL

TEXACO
REG. T.M.

TEXACO
REG. T.M.

DISTRIBUTOR
THE TEXAS
COMPANY

Diesel Chief

TEXACO

TEXACO
REG. T.M.

DIESEL
CHIEF
(DIESEL FUEL)

Chapter 5

Texaco Signs

Signs are probably the most popular Texaco collectible, simply because there are so many different styles available. This chapter lists the signs from all of the companies under the Texaco umbrella.

Texaco
Identification Signs
Texaco was the first gasoline brand to introduce a standardized, pole-mounted sign to identify its marketing facilities. Other companies had used building-mounted signs prior to this time, but with the invention of the off-street filling station by Gulf in 1913, the sales offices for filling stations were moved from the curb to a position at the back of a lot. To identify the facility, a pole-mounted sign was installed at street side, identifying the brand of gasoline sold there. Today's internally-illuminated, sectioned pylon identification signs have evolved from the original, single, 42" diameter, flat porcelain sign.

Texaco Filling Station
1915–1920 (5) 42" $2,000–3,500
The first Texaco identification sign. White outline around red outer ring. Black-outlined Texaco red star and black-outlined green "T" logo in center. Black "MOTOR OILS" across bottom of star. White

From gas pump signs to banjo signs to curb signs, Texaco offers everything for collectors.
Richard Eaves Collection

The first branded identification sign ever used in the petroleum industry is this 42" diameter porcelain Texaco Gasoline Filling Station sign introduced in 1915 and used through about 1920.

"GASOLINE" arched around top of red band, "FILLING STATION" arched around bottom.

Note: Two versions of this sign exits.
Texaco Gasoline/Motor Oil
1920–1936 (3) 42" $400–600
This Texaco sign became the standard identification sign around 1920 and remained at many locations into the postwar era. Black outline around red outer ring. Black-outlined Texaco red star and black-outlined green "T" logo in center. White

"Trust Your Car to the Man Who Wears the Star." "The Star that Shines All Night." "Star of the American Road." The Texaco "banjo" sign displays the star that nearly a century of motorists have looked to. Asheville, North Carolina, 1988.

"GASOLINE" arched around top of red band, "MOTOR OIL" arched around bottom. Black "MADE BY THE TEXAS COMPANY" arched around bottom of center, white logo area.

Texaco Gasoline
1932–1936 (5)   42" $400–600
A modified version of the earlier "GASOLINE/MO-TOR OIL" sign. White "TEXACO" arched around top of red border, "GASOLINE" around bottom. Extremely rare, and may have been an experimental replacement for the earlier sign.

Texaco (Reg. T.M.)
1936–1960 (1)   72" $150–250
The classic Texaco sign, introduced as part of the modernization of the Texaco image in 1936, and one of the first of the larger-generation identification signs, sometimes called "major signs." The sign is the image of the Texaco logo, with a black outline around a white circle. A large red star is in the center of the circle, with a white-outlined green "T" in the center of the star. Black "TEXACO" across top of star, and a small "REG. T.M." below the star. The introduction of this sign was the initial phase-in of the revised logo with the white border "T." This version is known with dates through 1960.

Texaco "R"
1960–1968 (1)   72" $150–250
Same as above, with the "circled R" (®) registered trademark image replacing "REG. T.M." at bottom of star. This version has been seen dated as early as 1960 and as late as 1968.

Texaco hexagon
1968–1982 (1)   48" x 96" $75–125
Black/white-outlined red hexagon logo with a white hexagon across the center. Black "TEXACO" across center, with a small "red star and green T" logo at the bottom center of the red area.

Texaco hexagon
1968–1982 (3)   48" x 96" $50–100
Fiberglass version of the sign listed above. Black/white-outlined red hexagon logo with a white hexagon across the center. Black "TEXA-CO" across center, with a small "red star and green T" logo at the bottom center of the red area.

Texaco
1982–present (5) 72"   no listing
Several examples of these signs were custom-made for locations where zoning laws prevented existing sign structures from being removed and replaced. The existing banjo pole was fitted with a baked-enamel, red, circular aluminum sign with an adhesive vinyl white star in the image of the new "white star" logo.

Illuminated Signs
Texaco used various examples of illuminated signage prior to its image standardization of the late 1930s, but much of this early signage was structural, and too large to be considered collectible. Texaco was one of the last major oil companies to introduce and commonly use internally-illuminated identification signs.

Texaco
1960–1968 (5) 72" $150–250
In the early 1960s, Texaco finally introduced an internally-illuminated version of its classic sign, and was one of the last major oil companies to do so. These were used only at some high-visibility locations, and many were soon replaced with the newer hexagon logo. They were mounted on the standard "banjo" pole.

Texaco canopy sign
1982–present (2) 36" $150–250
The current canopy sign is already popular among collectors. Assembled metal sign cabinet with internal light fixtures. Red plastic face with white star logo in center.

Sign Poles
Only recently considered collectible, more and more collectors are choosing to display their signs on original poles. Many early poles are very ornate, although all are very heavy and awkward to display in any but rural areas.

Texaco shepherds crook pole
1920–1936 (4) 10'+/- $150–250
Simple pipe pole, with a curved top section encircling the sign in the upper section, forming the appearance of a "question mark."

Interstate highways demanded signage to attract motorists' attention at great distances. The Texaco modular high-rise was developed in the early-1960s to identify Texaco Interstate locations. This example stood beside a Stuckey's Texaco outlet at Old Fort, North Carolina, in 1988.

Texaco Denver pole
1926–1936 (5) 12'+/- $350–500
Ornate cast iron pole with pipe mast arm and wrought iron support scrollwork.

Texaco banjo pole
1936–1968 (1) 18' $75–150
The classic Texaco sign pole, an American icon. Assembled steel-plate pole with circular angle iron sign frame in a single welded assembly. Despite being discontinued in 1968, many remain in use even today.

Texaco side-mount pole
1955–1968 (4) 18' $75–150
An unusual pole used to display the classic Texaco sign. Welded steel plate upright with two support arms curved outward at top of pole to attach angle-iron circular sign frame. Used in areas where sign had to project outward for visibility.

Texaco trucks delivering "Clean, Clear, Golden Texaco Motor Oil" advertised their wares with door signage like the beautiful example shown here. *Dunbar's Gallery*

Texaco hexagon center pole
1968–1982 (2)   18' $50–75
This welded steel pole and angle-iron frame for the hexagon signs is not overly popular among collectors.

Texaco hexagon side-mount pole
1968–1982 (2)   16' $75–125
A welded steel plate pole or unusual design, tapering bottom to top. Angle-iron sign frame is bolted to side of pole at the top, with top edge curving down to pole to give appearance of single structure.

Building Signs and Letters
Texaco porcelain
1938–1950 (5)   18" $350–550/set
Individual, red formed porcelain, deep-channel letters spelling "TEXACO."

Texaco plastic
1950–1968 (2)   12" & 18" $50–100/set
Individual, red cast plastic, deep-channel letters spelling "TEXACO."

Texaco plastic
1968–1970 (2)   12" & 18" $35–50/set
Individual, black cast plastic, deep-channel letters spelling "TEXACO."

Texaco porcelain star
1938–1950 (3)   16" $100–150
Red, three-dimensional, formed porcelain star for use on building exteriors.

Texaco plastic star
1950–1968 (2)   16" $20–35
Red, three-dimensional, formed porcelain star for use on building exteriors.

Texaco plastic star
1968–1970 (2)   16" $20–35
Black, three-dimensional, formed porcelain star for use on building exteriors.

Texaco green letters
1938–1968 (2)   6" $2 each
Used for secondary lettering on station buildings. All individual letters and symbols known. Green cast plastic.

Texaco utility signs were used for many purposes, from bulk oil lubesters to truck doors. The earlier example displays a black border "T" and is dated "4-30." The larger, white border "T" sign is the newer of the pair. *Richard Eaves Collection*

The most familiar signs to collectors of petroleum memorabilia are the simple Texaco Fire Chief and Texaco Sky Chief designs. Multiple colors and details of the fireman's hat add to the beauty of the Fire Chief sign, while the contrasting red, green, and black art-deco design adds appeal to the Sky Chief example. *Richard Eaves Collection*

Later versions of the Texaco Diesel Chief signs displayed much thinner rays, and white lettering at the bottom. Diesel Chief "L" was a special product marketed by Texaco in this era. *Richard Eaves Collection*

Sky Chief was Texaco's premium grade fuel, and in 1954 the additive "Petrox" was introduced to enhance Sky Chief gasoline. Some existing pump signs were converted with the addition of a small strip with the white and red bands at the bottom, while new installations received large (12" x 22.5") porcelain examples like the ones shown here. *Richard Eaves Collection*

Texaco stained glass window
1918–1942 (4)   22" $1,000–1,500
Sign installed in building eaves. Lead channel framework for stained glass (colors) and milk glass (white area) lenses in the image of the Texaco logo. One of the most unique gasoline signs ever created. Used as late as the

Specialty Diesel products were advertised by these two pump signs. Fuel Chief 1 was Texaco Diesel Fuel sold for home heating purposes, and Diesel Fuel 2 was Texaco's regular grade product.
Richard Eaves Collection

early-1940s on some prototype Teague Texaco stations.. Nineteen and 28" versions also exist.

Texaco stripe panels
1950–1970 (3) 12" wide $25–35 each
Porcelain over aluminum panels forming three parallel green stripes with white section between. Used for installation on station buildings of nonstandard construction to create the Texaco image.

Texaco dealer nameplate
1926–1938 (5) 12" x 48" +/- $75–125
Brown rectangular panel with rounded ends. Gold letters across center, custom made for dealer or station identification name.

Flat Pump Signs
Drain And Refill Texaco Motor Oil
1926–1930 (4) 15" $250–300
Gray-outlined, black porcelain sign with white band across top. Black "DRAIN/AND REFILL WITH" on white area. White "Clean, Clear," over yellow "GOLDEN," over white "TEXACO/MOTOR/OIL" on lower black area beside gray pitcher with yellow oil pouring to left of lettering.

Texaco (black border T)
1930–1943 (4) 7" $200–250

Texaco (black border T)
1930–1943 (2) 8" $200–250

Texaco (black border T)
1930–1943 (4) 10" $200–250

Texaco (black border T)
1930–1943 (3) 15" $200–250
These signs are commonly referred to as utility signs, as they were used not only for pump panels, but for trucks, buildings, and any miscellaneous purpose necessary. A round sign, in the image of the classic Texaco logo. Black outline around white circle. Large red star in center with a black-outlined green "T" in the center. Black "TEXACO" across top of star. Some sizes of these signs are known to be dated as late as 1943 or 1944.

Texaco (white border T)
1943–1968 (3) 8" $200–250
These signs are commonly referred to as utility signs, as they were for trucks, buildings, and any miscellaneous purpose necessary. By the time the revised white border "T" logo was introduced, they were no longer used on gas pumps. These are round signs, in the image of the classic Texaco logo. Black outline around white circle. Large red star in center with a white-outlined green "T" in the center. Black "TEXACO" across top of star. The earliest dates to appear on these signs are 1943 or 1944..

Note: The utility signs listed above were not used for gasoline pump identification after the early 1930s, although they remained in use on kerosene dispensers and in other assorted uses. Decals were used on Texaco Fire Chief and Texaco Fire Chief Ethyl gas pumps from 1932 until 1939. Several different images were used. Beginning in 1939, standardized pump signs for all products were introduced, and they—in three different standard sizes—would remain in specifications until 1968. Many are still found on pumps in remote locations, even today. The signs that are 12" x 18" were the standard size, used on most regular service station pumps. The smaller versions that are 8" x 12" were used on pumps with narrow doors, on the sides of pumps in states where display of a state or local license was required on the front doors of regular service station pumps, some visible pumps remaining in use, portable gasoline carts, and other unusual applications. The mid-size 10" x 15" signs were used on two-product twin pumps of the 1950s and 1960s, and they are the hardest to find.

Regular Grade "Fire Chief Gasoline"
Fire Chief
1939–1968 (1) 12" x 18" $40–75

Fire Chief
1959–1968 (4) 10" x 15" $100–150

Fire Chief
1939–1968 (4) 8" x 12" $125–175
The largest version is probably the most commonly found petroleum collectible of all time. Black-outlined white porcelain sign with a large, red fireman's hat in center. Circular Texaco logo at left of hat, with red "FIRE CHIEF" across top, above black "GASOLINE." Known dates from 1939 until 1968, and decals of this same image known dated as late as 1971.

Premium Grade "Sky Chief Gasoline"
Sky Chief
1939–1955 (1) 12" x 18" $40–75

Sky Chief
1939–1955 (4) 8" x 12" $100–150
Green porcelain sign with black, one third-height band across bottom, and series of green and white stripes across top. Black-outlined red "wing" logo with Texaco logo in center, covers most of sign face. Black-outlined white band across top with red "SKY CHIEF" across band. White "GASOLINE" across bottom.

Sky Chief Petrox
1955–1959 (3) 12" x 22.5" $100–125

Sky Chief Petrox
1955–1959 (4) 12" x 18" $125–150
Green porcelain sign with black, one third-height band across lower center, and series of green and white stripes across top. Black-outlined red "wing" logo with Texaco logo in center, covers most of sign face. Black-outlined white band across top with red "SKY CHIEF" across band. White

The design of the Texaco hexagon logo was adopted for these pump signs used between 1968 and 1971. These are made of embossed lithographed tin, and examples in good condition are quite rare.
Richard Eaves Collection

Texaco products sold at landing strips were advertised by this 30" diameter porcelain Texaco Aviation Products curb sign that dates from around 1930.
Collectors Auction Service

This beautiful multi-color curb sign was used in the late 1920s to advertise Texaco's "Clean, Clear, Golden Motor Oil." *Richard Eaves Collection*

"GASOLINE" across bottom of black band. White band over red band below black area, with red script "SUPER CHARGED WITH" on white band and white "PETROX" on red band.

Sky Chief Su-Preme
1959–1968 (1)   12" x 18" $40–75

Sky Chief Su-Preme
1959–1968 (4)   10" x 15" $100–150

Sky Chief Su-Preme
1959–1968 (4)   8" x 12" $125–175
Green porcelain sign with white band across top and bottom. Black-outlined red "wing" logo with Texaco logo in center, covers most of sign face. Red "SKY CHIEF" over black "SU-PREME" in top band, black "SUPER CHARGED WITH" over red "PETROX" in bottom band.

Motor Grade "Indian Gasoline"
Indian
1939–1946 (2)   12" x 18" $200–250

Indian
1939–1946 (3)   8" x 12" $300–350
Green porcelain sign with blue lower half. White "INDIAN" over green "GASOLINE" on lower blue area. Multicolor "Indian bead" motif with teepees on upper green area.

Premium Diesel Grade Diesel Chief
Diesel Chief (black)
1939–1945 (5)   12" x 18" $800–1,000
White porcelain sign with red lower half. Red injector nozzle projecting into upper white area with thick red lines forming spray image covering white area. Large Texaco logo superimposed over spray at top. Black "DIESEL/CHIEF" over white "(DIESEL FUEL)" on lower red area. An extremely rare sign that was modified at the end of World War II because of its similarity in appearance to the Japanese rising sun image.

Diesel Chief (red)
1945–1968 (3) 12" x 18" $150–200

Diesel Chief (red)
1945–1968 (4) 8" x 12" $325–400
White porcelain sign with red lower half. Red in-

jector nozzle projecting into upper white area with thin, red lines forming spray image covering white area. Large Texaco logo superimposed over spray at top. White "DIESEL/CHIEF" over black "(DIESEL FUEL)" on lower red area.

Diesel Chief shield
1968–1971 (3) 10" x 15" $150–250
Die-cut embossed tin litho hexagon with green outer band and white center. Black-outlined white Texaco "red star and green T" logo at bottom center of green band. Black "Diesel Chief" across center of white area.

Regular Diesel Grade "Diesel Fuel #2"
Diesel Fuel #2
1945–1968 (3) 12" x 18" $250–300

Diesel Fuel #2
1945–1968 (4) 8" x 12" $350–450
White porcelain sign with green lower half. Green injector nozzle projecting into upper white area with thin, green lines forming spray image covering white area. Large Texaco logo superimposed over spray at top. White "DIESEL/FUEL 2" on lower green area.

Special Diesel Grade "Diesel Chief L"
Diesel Chief "L"
1955–1965 (5) 12" x 18" $400–650
White porcelain sign with red lower half. Red injector nozzle projecting into upper white area with thin, red lines forming spray image covering white area. Large Texaco logo superimposed over spray at top. White "DIESEL/CHIEF L" over black "(DIESEL FUEL)" on lower red area.

Specific Auto Diesel Grade
Auto Diesel
1965–1968 (5) 12" x 18" $200–300
White tin litho sign with red lower half. Red injector nozzle projecting into upper white area with thin, red lines forming spray image covering white area. Large round Texaco logo superimposed over spray at top. White "AUTO/DIESEL" on lower red area.

Auto Diesel
1968–1971 (5) 12" x 18" $200–300
White tin litho sign with red lower half. Red injector nozzle projecting into upper white area with thin, red

Motor oil racks were often adorned with unusual signs, but few were anywhere near as decorative as this late-1950s sign advertising Texaco Outboard Products. *Richard Eaves Collection*

lines forming spray image covering white area. Large hexagon Texaco logo superimposed over spray at top. White "AUTO/DIESEL" on lower red area.

Heating Oil For Home Heating
Fuel Chief
1963–1968 (5) 12" x 18" $750–850
White porcelain sign with yellow lower half. Yellow injector nozzle projecting into upper white area with thin, yellow lines forming spray image covering white area. Large Texaco logo superimposed over spray at top. Black "FUEL/CHIEF" over red "(DIESEL FUEL)" on lower yellow area.

Leaded Grade Marine Fuel
Sky Chief Marine
1946–1955 (4) 12" x 18" $225–325

Sky Chief Marine
1946–1955 (5) 8" x 12" $400–650
Green porcelain sign with black, one third-height band across bottom, and series of green and white stripes across top. Black-outlined red "wing" logo with Texaco logo in center, covers most of sign face. Black-outlined white band across top with red "Sky Chief " over red "MARINE" across band. White "GASOLINE" across bottom.

One of the most unusual of all Texaco lubricants signage is the Marine Lubricants sign used in the 1960s. It replaced the earlier and more decorative "ships and gulls" signage that shared a design with product packaging. Also shown here are several of the most desirable of the many Texaco pump signs, the Marine White signs used from the 1940s until 1968. Both the standard 12" x 18" sign and the smaller 8" x 12" version are shown. *Richard Eaves Collection*

Sky Chief Marine Petrox
1955–1968   (3)   12" x 22.5" $225–400

Sky Chief Marine Petrox
1955–1968   (5)   12" x 18" $250–450

Sky Chief Marine Petrox
1955–1968   (5)   8" x 12" $300–600
Green porcelain sign with black, one third-height band across bottom, and series of green and white stripes across top. Black-outlined red "wing" logo with Texaco logo in center, covers most of sign face. Black-outlined white band across top with red "Sky Chief " over black "MARINE" across band. White "GASOLINE" across bottom. White band over red band below black area, with red script "SUPER CHARGED WITH" on white band and white "PETROX" on red band.

Sea Chief
1968–1971   (4)   10" x 15" $150–250
Die-cut embossed tin litho hexagon with gold outer band and white center. Black-outlined white Texaco "red star and green T" logo at bottom center of gold band. Black "Sea Chief" across center of white area.

Unleaded Grade Marine Fuel
Marine White
1945–1968   (3)   12" x 18" $750–1,000

Marine White
1945–1968   (5)   10" x 15" $850–1,100

Marine White
1945–1968   (4)   8" x 12" $900–1,400
Green porcelain sign with black lower half. Large Texaco "red star and green T" logo encircled by red and white "ship's wheel" on upper green area. White/black "rope" design script "MARINE/WHITE" above red "GASOLINE" on lower black area.

Marine White shield
1968–1971   (5)   10" x 15" $150–250
Die-cut embossed tin litho hexagon with red outer band and white center. Black-outlined white Texaco "red star and green T" logo at bottom center of red band. Black "Marine White" across center of white area.

Gasoline/Oil Mixture For Outboard Engines
Texaco Outboard Blend
1965–1968   (5)   12" x 18" $150–200
White horizontal-format porcelain sign with green outer border version of Texaco hexagon logo. Small, red star and green "T" at bottom of logo border. Red "TEXACO" across logo. Black "OUT-BOARD BLEND" across bottom of sign.

Texaco Outboard Blend
1968–1971   (5)   12" x 18" $100–150
White horizontal-format porcelain sign with normal red outer border version of Texaco hexagon logo. Small, red star and green "T" at bottom of logo border. Normal black "TEXACO" across logo. Black "OUTBOARD BLEND" across bottom of sign.

Curved Pump Signs
Drain And Refill Texaco Motor Oil
1926–1930   (4)   15" $275–350
Curved, gray-outlined, black porcelain sign with white band across top. Black "DRAIN/AND RE-FILL WITH" on white area. White "Clean, Clear," over yellow "GOLDEN," over white "TEXACO/MOTOR/OIL" on lower black area beside gray pitcher with yellow oil pouring to left of lettering.

Texaco (black border T)
1930–1943   (4)   7" $200–250

Texaco (black border T)
1930–1943   (2)   8" $200–250

Texaco (black border T)
1930–1943   (3)   15" $200–250
While flat examples are considered "utility" signs used for multiple purposes, the curved versions were made specifically to fit on round gas pumps. A circular sign in the image of the classic Texaco logo. Black outline around white circle. Large red star in center with a black-outlined green "T" in the center. Black "TEXACO" across top of star. Some sizes of these signs are known to be dated as late as 1943 or 1944.

Regular Grade "Fire Chief Gasoline"
Fire Chief
1939–1968   (1)   12" x 18" $75–100

This early Havoline porcelain oil rack sign promotes the newly introduced sealed quart cans that Texaco began using in 1934. *Leelan Glanzer*

Fire Chief
1939–1968 (2)   8" x 12" $150–200
Curved, black-outlined, white porcelain sign with a large red fireman's hat in center. Circular Texaco logo at left of hat, with red "FIRE CHIEF" across top above black "GASOLINE." Known dates from 1939 until 1968, and decals of this same image known dated as late as 1971.

Premium Grade "Sky Chief Gasoline"
Sky Chief
1939–1955 (1)   12" x 18" $75–100

Sky Chief
1939–1955 (2)   8" x 12" $150–200
Curved, green porcelain sign with black one-third-height band across bottom, and series of green and white stripes across top. Black-outlined red "wing" logo with Texaco logo in center, covers most of sign face. Black-outlined white band across top with red "SKY CHIEF" across band. White "GASOLINE" across bottom.

Motor Grade "Indian Gasoline"
Indian
1939–1946 (2)   12" x 18" $175–250

Indian
1939–1946 (3)   8" x 12" $250–325
Curved, green porcelain sign with blue lower half. White "INDIAN" over green "GASOLINE" on lower blue area. Multicolor "Indian bead" motif with teepees on upper green area.

Unleaded Grade Marine Fuel
Marine White
1945–1968 (3)   12" x 18" $350–500
Curved, green porcelain sign with black lower half. Large Texaco "red star and green T" logo encircled by red and white "ship's wheel" on upper green area. White/black "rope" design script "MARINE/WHITE" above red "GASOLINE" on lower black area.

Neon Signs
Texaco plastic neon letters
1955–1970 (4)   various $300–500
Individual channel letters mounted on a porcelain base. The channels were filled with shaped neon, and thick red plastic lenses covered the channels, resulting in a set of individual red letters. They were mounted on canopy edges and other rooftop locations. Known assembled on either a single 12' strip or on two strips totaling 16'.

Curb Signs
Texaco Filling Station
1915–1920 (7)   30"   no listing
The first Texaco identification sign. White outline around red outer ring. Black-outlined Texaco red star and black-outlined green "T" logo in center. Black "MOTOR OILS" across bottom of star. White "GASOLINE" arched around top of red band, "FILLING STATION" arched around bottom.

Texaco Motor Oil
1920–1925 (5)   30"   no listing
Black outline around red outer ring. Black-outlined Texaco red star and black-outlined green "T" logo in center. White "TEXACO" arched around top of red band, "MOTOR OIL" arched around bottom. Black "MADE BY THE TEXAS COMPANY" arched around bottom of center white logo area.

Texaco Ethyl
1926–1932 (4)   30" $500–850
Red porcelain sign with black-outlined white Texaco "red star and black-outlined T" logo at top, over black-outlined white circle with large yellow and blue ethyl sign below.

Texaco Certified Service

1920s (4) 30" x 30" $200–275
White porcelain square sign with angled corners with red band across just above center. White "CERTIFIED" on red band with red "TEXACO" above and "SERVICE" below. Smaller red lettering across bottom.

Texaco Motor Oil
1920s–1934 (2) 30" x 30" $350–450
White square sign with angled corners. Large, black-outlined red "TEXACO/MOTOR OIL" across top, above black rectangular octagon. Gray pitcher pouring yellow motor oil on black area with motto "CLEAN/ CLEAR/GOLDEN" to side, above red-outlined Texaco logo.

New - New Texaco Motor Oil
1936–1939 (5) 30" x 30" $150–250
Green tin litho square sign with angled corners with red and white Texaco "New Texaco Motor Oil" can in center of sign. Large, black-outlined, white "NEW" across top of sign.

Insulated Texaco Motor Oil
1939–1942 (5) 30" x 30" $150–250
Black tin litho square sign with angled corners with red and white Texaco "TEXACO MOTOR OIL-INSULATED" can in center of sign. Large, red "INSULATED" across top of sign.

Havoline Motor Oil
1939–1942 (5) 30" x 30" $200–250
Porcelain square sign with angled corners has white upper half and blue lower half. Blue/white-outlined red dot in center at color split. White logotype "HAVOLINE/ MOTOR OIL" with red "DIS-TILLED INSULATED" on lower blue area, with red "KEEPS YOUR ENGINE CLEAN" across top.

Texaco Sky Chief
1939–1942 (5) 30" $450–600
Green tin litho sign with black one third-height band across bottom, and series of green and white stripes across top. Black-outlined red "wing" logo with Texaco logo in center, covers most of sign face. Black-outlined white band across top with red "SKY CHIEF" across band. White "GASO-LINE" across bottom. All known are dated 1939.

Texaco Aviation

Havoline Motor Oils were sold in sealed cans from a rack that displayed this sign in the 1940s.
Leelan Glanzer

1930–1935 (5) 24" no listing
Red outer band around black-outlined Texaco logo in center. Black border around "T" on star. Black-outlined white "AVIATION" arched around top, "PRODUCTS" around bottom.

Lubrication Signs
Easy Pour Can 2 Qts Texaco Motor Oil
1922–1927 (4) 13" x 13" $1,800–2,500
White/black-outlined porcelain sign with green/white/red two-quart can on square with black "EASY POUR/CAN" above and red "2" black "QTS" above black "TEXACO/MOTOR OIL" below.

Easy Pour Can 2 Qts Texaco Motor Oil
1922–1927 (5) 13" x 13" $1,800–2,500
White/black-outlined porcelain sign with black/white/red two-quart can on square with black "EASY POUR/CAN" above and red "2" black "QTS" above black "TEXACO/MOTOR OIL" below.
Texaco Certified Lubrication

These Texaco "keyhole" signs were designed for use on truck doors. Local distributor or agent name could be painted in, or custom porcelain examples could be ordered by the distributor. *Richard Eaves Collection*

1920s   (4)   9" x 39" $250–300
White porcelain sign with Texaco logo (black-outlined "T") at either end. Black-outlined red "TEXACO/CERTIFIED LUBRICATION" above black "IN ACCORDANCE WITH APPROVED PRACTICE" between logos.

Texaco Crankcase Service
1928–1930 (4)   22" x 28" $225–275
Black, square-dotted border around white porcelain sign. Black-outlined Texaco logo (black border "T") at top over black "CRANKCASE/SERVICE." Red "LET US DRAIN YOUR CRANKCASE AND/REFILL WITH CLEAN, CLEAR, GOLDEN (in yellow)." Gray-outlined white "TEXACO/MOTOR/OIL" below.

Clean, Clear Golden Texaco Motor Oil
1928–1934 (5)   10" x 10" $450–550
White-outlined black porcelain sign with gold stream of motor oil on left side. White "CLEAN,/CLEAR" across top of black area above yellow "GOLDEN." Gray-outlined white "TEXACO/MOTOR/OIL" below.

Clean, Clear Golden Texaco Motor Oil
1928–1934 (3)   14" x 14" $350–450
White-outlined black porcelain sign with gold stream of motor oil on left side. White "Clean,/Clear" across top of black area above yellow "GOLDEN." Gray-outlined white "TEXACO/MOTOR/OIL" below.

Marfak Lubrication
1946–1960 (2)   24" x 40" $150–200
Black-outlined white tin litho sign with red band diagonal across center. White "MARFAK" on band with Texaco logo above and black script "Lubrication" below.

Let Us Marfak Your Car
1934–1946 (3)   24" x 40" $150–200
Black-outlined white tin litho sign with red band diagonal across center. White "MARFAK" on band with black script "LET US" above and black script "YOUR CAR" below.

New Texaco Motor Oil Furfural'd
1937–1938 (5)   18" x 30" $500–650
Detailed sign with attendant holding dip stick with red and black "NEW TEXACO MOTOR OIL" can to right side. Black "STAYS FULL (red) LONGER" across center with white "THE FURFURAL'd FILM DOES IT!" on blue band across bottom. Originals are tin litho and are dated 2/37. Porcelain and tin litho reproductions have been made.

Lubester Signs
Texaco Motor Oil
1915–1934 (3)   5" $350–500
Circular porcelain sign with black mounting tab at the bottom. Red outer border area around black-outlined Texaco star logo. Black-outlined "T" in star. White "TEXACO" arched around top of red area, "MOTOR OIL" around bottom. Black "MADE BY THE TEXAS COMPANY U.S.A." arched around inside bottom of logo.

Texaco Motor Oil/Fords
1915–1930 (4)   3" x 12" $200–225
Black-outlined white porcelain sign with black "TEXACO MOTOR OIL" across top. Smaller "FORDS" across bottom.

Oil Rack Signs
Custom-designed oil can racks were used by Texaco from the 1934 introduction of sealed cans until the early 1950s. Other, later, tin litho signs are known that were used on "Seloil" cabinets in the 1950s and 1960s, but the signs listed below are the classic Texaco oil rack signs, designed to match cans of the same era.

New Texaco Motor Oil
1934–1940 (5)   11" x 21" $200–250
Porcelain sign in style of checkerboard can. Red over white square to right, white over red square to left. Large Texaco logo (black outline "T") on each red field, with black "TEXACO/MOTOR OIL" on each white field. Black-outlined green band diagonal in center, lettered "NEW."

Havoline Motor Oil - Waxfree
1934–1940 (3)   11" x 21" $200–250
Porcelain sign has white upper half and blue lower half. Blue/white-outlined red dot in center at color split. White logotype "HAVOLINE/MOTOR OIL" on lower blue area above red "WAXFREE," with blue "REFINERY/SEALED CANS" to left of dot, "FOR YOUR/PROTECTION" to right. Dated 6/34, to correspond to the introduction of sealed cans.

Texaco Motor Oil - Insulated
1940–1946 (3)   11" x 14" $200–250
White porcelain sign with red band across top. Texaco logo centered on band with white-outlined "T" in star. Green "TEXACO/MOTOR OIL" on white area above red "INSULATED." Small green "AGAINST HEAT AGAINST COLD" across bottom below "INSULATED."

Havoline Motor Oil
1940–1946 (4)   11" x 14" $200–250
Porcelain sign has white upper half and blue lower half. Blue/white-outlined red dot in center at color split. White logotype "HAVOLINE/MOTOR OIL" on lower blue area, with red "KEEPS YOUR" to left of dot, "ENGINE CLEAN" to right.

Texaco Motor Oil - Insulated
1947–1953 (2)   11" x 21" $200–250
Tin litho sign in style of checkerboard can. Red over white square to right, white over red square to left. Large Texaco logo (white outline "T") on each red field, with Black "TEXACO/MOTOR OIL" in each white field. Green and white band diagonal in center lettered "AGAINST HEAT/INSULATED/ AGAINST COLD."

Havoline Motor Oil

1946–1953 (3) 11" x 21" $200–250
Tin litho sign has white upper half and blue lower half. Blue/white-outlined red dot in center at color split. White logotype "HAVOLINE/MOTOR OIL" on lower blue area, with red "KEEPS YOUR" to left of dot, "ENGINE CLEAN" to right. Red "NEW AND/IMPROVED" at upper left above dot.

Texaco Marine Lubricants w/boats
1950s–1962 (4) 11" x 21" $1,800–2,500
White porcelain sign with green band across top and green band across bottom representing water in a harbor scene. Assorted boats in red, white, and black on "water" at bottom, black-outlined white seagulls in upper green area. Black-outlined white Texaco logo with red star and white-outlined green "T" at upper left and upper right of center white area. Black-outlined red "TEXA-CO" arched between logos, with black "MA-RINE LUBRICANTS" below.
Note: Examples of this sign, dated 1947, with a black-outlined "T" in the two logos, dated 1947, are known. It is believed that most of these are reproductions yet a few originals do exist of the Black Outlined "T."

Secondary Signs
Texaco No Smoking (white/black)
1915–1930 (4) 6" x 24" $1,500–1,800
White-outlined black porcelain sign with red-bordered Texaco logo at each end. White "THE TEXAS COMPANY U.S.A." arched in red area around top of logo, "PETROLEUM PRODUCTS" below. Large white "NO SMOKING" across sign between logos.

No Smoking The Texas Company
1920s–1930s (3) 6" x 12" $175–275
Black-outlined white sign with large black "NO SMOKING" across center. Smaller, black "THE TEXAS COMPANY" across the bottom.

Texaco No Smoking (black border T)
1930–1944 (2) 4" x 23" $200–250
Black-outlined white porcelain strip with Texaco logo (black-outlined "T") at each end. Black "NO SMOKING" across center. Although it was highly unusual for any signage to be manufactured during World War II, this writer personally removed a Texaco No Smoking sign with a black-outlined green "T" on each logo from the

wall of a bulk plant in Minnesota. The reverse side of the sign was dated 1944, and it obviously had been installed there about that time. It can only be assumed that since a "no smoking" sign was essential for safety, that some were made up during the war for Texaco facilities that were opened then, perhaps in areas critical for national defense. The collector who purchased the sign just mentioned found another, within 60 days, at a plant in Georgia that also was dated 1944 on the back and had a white-outlined green "T" on each logo.

Texaco No Smoking (white border T)
1944–1968 (2) 4" x 23" $200–250
Black-outlined white porcelain strip with Texaco logo (white-outlined "T") at each end. Black "NO SMOKING" across center.

Texaco No Smoking (new logo)
1962–1982 (3) 4" x 23" $100–150
White porcelain strip with Texaco hexagon logo in red, black, and white at left end of sign. Black "NO SMOKING" to right of logo.

Texaco Mail Port
1950s (4) 17" x 23" $300–350
White porcelain sign with yellow and blue/white/red marine signal flags on pole at left. Red "TEXACO" over black "MAIL/PORT" across sign face.

Buy The Best, Buy Texaco
1946–1960 (4) 24" x 40" $175–225
Green-outlined tin litho sign with red upper half and white lower half. Green block on upper red band. Black script "Buy the Best" across red area extending into green box with red "BUY TEXACO" across lower white half. Small Texaco logo (white-outlined "T") to left of green block at color split.

Texaco Kerosene, Clean Burning
1940–1950s (4) 12" x 20" $150–200
White, flat tin litho sign with blue band across bottom. Blue oil "jets" with lighter blue flame projecting from jets across bottom area at color split. Red "TEXACO" across top above blue "KEROSENE." White "CLEAR" and red "BURNING" across bottom blue band.

Texaco Kerosine Clean Burning

1950s–1960s (3) 12" x 20" $150–200
White, embossed tin litho sign with blue band across bottom. Blue oil "jets" with lighter blue flame projecting from jets across bottom area at color split. Red "TEXACO" across top above blue "KEROSINE." White "CLEAR" and red "BURNING" across bottom blue band.

Rest Room Signs
Registered Rest Room
1937–1940 (3) 20" x 36" $75–100
White tin litho sign with green, colonial-style border projecting at top and smooth at bottom, with green edge line up each side. White "REGISTERED" in upper green area with large black "REST ROOM" in center. Smaller, black "A TEXACO DEALER SERVICE" across bottom.

Registered Rest Room
1940–1973 (3) 20" x 36" $75–100
White tin litho sign with green, colonial-style border smooth at top and smooth at bottom, with green edge line up each side. White "REGISTERED" in upper green area with large black "REST ROOM" in center. Smaller, white "A TEXACO DEALER SERVICE" across bottom green area.

Locked For Your Protection
1936–1968 (4) 6" x 6" $75–100
Black-outlined white porcelain sign with black "LOCKED/FOR YOUR/PROTECTION" across center.
Men
1936–1968 (3) 5" x 15" $35–50
White porcelain flange sign with three green stripes and green "MEN."

Ladies
1936–1968 (3) 5" x 15" $35–50
White porcelain flange sign with three green stripes and green "LADIES."

Men die cut
1968–1973 (4) 6" x 15" $25–35
Yellow tin litho die cut flange sign in the shape of the Texaco hexagon. Olive green "MEN" across sign.

Ladies die cut
1968–1973 (4) 6" x 15" $25–35

With fire an ever-present danger in petroleum storage, employees and customers are reminded that "no smoking" was allowed. Various "No Smoking" signs used by Texaco have become highly collectible. *Richard Eaves Collection*

Yellow tin litho die cut flange sign in the shape of the Texaco hexagon. Olive green "LADIES" across sign.

Flange Signs
Easy Pour Can
1922–1925 (4) 12" x 18" $1,800–2,800
Red porcelain flange sign with black-outlined white square at top. Green/white/red two quart can on square with black "EASY POUR/CAN" above, "TWO QUARTS" below. Black-outlined white "TEXACO/MOTOR OIL" above smaller lettering below square.

Clean, Clear Golden Texaco Motor Oil
1928–1933 (4) 12" x 16" $750–850
Black porcelain flange tombstone-shaped sign with

Texaco gasolines were custom blended for use in specific regions of the country, because temperature, atmospheric pressure, and altitude would affect automobile performance. Texaco advertised the practice with signs like these displayed on pump islands or pump tops. *Richard Eaves Collection*

gold stream of motor oil on left side. White "CLEAN, CLEAR" across top of black area above yellow "GOLDEN." Gray-outlined white "TEXACO/MOTOR/OIL" below. Small red-outlined Texaco star logo at top.

Clean, Clear Golden Texaco Motor Oil
1928–1933 (5) 12" x 18" $450–600
Red-outlined white porcelain sign with black/white-outlined vertical rectangle with cut corners in center. Silver can pouring gold oil through center of black area. White "CLEAN, CLEAR" above yellow "GOLDEN" and small red-outlined Texaco star logo beside oil. Black "TEXA-

CO/ MOTOR OIL" across sign below black area.
New Texaco Motor Oil
1934–1939 (4) 13" x 20" $300–500
Die-cut red/white/black tin flange sign replica of 1934 "NEW TEXACO MOTOR OIL" can.

Havoline Waxfree Motor Oil
1934–1939 (4) 13" x 20" $1,200–1,500
Die-cut red/white/blue porcelain flange sign replica of 1934 "HAVOLINE MOTOR OIL - WAXFREE" can.

The Texas Company, USA Petroleum
Products Texaco Motor Oil

1915–1920s (4) 23" x 18" $900–1,200

Perhaps the most popular of the Texaco flange signs. Die-cut black porcelain flange sign with large red-bordered white Texaco red star and black-outlined green "T" logo at top. Black-outlined white "THE TEXAS COMPANY U.S.A." arched around top on red band, "PETROLEUM PRODUCTS" below. White "TEXACO/MOTOR OIL" on black area below logo.

Truck Signs

Texaco, The Texas Company
1930–1946 (5) 10.5" x 12.5" $300–350
Keyhole-shaped, die-cut, black-outlined white porcelain sign. Texaco logo with red star and black-outlined green "T" at top. Black "THE TEXAS/ COMPANY" on lower part of sign.

Texaco Agent
1930–1946 (4) 10.5" x 15.5" $300–350
Keyhole-shaped, die-cut, black-outlined white porcelain sign. Texaco logo with red star and black-outlined green "T" at top. Blank area to paint in distributor name above black "AGENT/THE TEXAS/ COMPANY" on lower part of sign.

Texaco Distributor
1930–1946 (4) 10.5" x 15.5" $300–350
Keyhole shaped, die-cut, black-outlined white porcelain sign. Texaco logo with red star and black-outlined green "T" at top. Blank area to paint in distributor name above black "DISTRIBUTOR/THE TEXAS/ COMPANY" on lower part of sign.

Texaco, The Texas Company
1946–1959 (5) 10.5" x 12.5" $300–350
Keyhole-shaped, die-cut, black-outlined white porcelain sign. Texaco logo with red star and black-outlined green "T" at top. Black "THE TEXAS/ COMPANY" on lower part of sign.

Texaco Consignee
1946–1968 (4) 10.5" x 12.5" $300–350
Keyhole-shaped, die-cut, black-outlined white porcelain sign. Texaco logo with red star and black-outlined green "T" at top. Black distributor name above black "CONSIGNEE" on lower part of sign.

Texaco Distributor
1946–1968 (3) 10.5" x 12.5" $300–350
Keyhole-shaped, die-cut, black-outlined white porcelain sign. Texaco logo with red star and white-outlined green "T" at top. Black distributor name above black "DISTRIBUTOR" on lower part of sign.

Texaco
1935–1946 (5) 24" $300–350
Sign for back door of truck. Black-outlined Texaco logo sign with red star and black-outlined green "T." Black "TEXACO" across top of star.

Texaco
1946–1968 (5) 24" $300–350
Sign for back door of truck. Black-outlined Texaco logo sign with red star and white-outlined green "T." Black "TEXACO" across top of star.

Texaco Lettering
1930s (4) 12" $200–250/set
Individual black-outlined white letters spelling "TEXACO." Installed on side or back of tank truck.

Gasoline lettering
1930s (5) 6" $75–100/set
Individual black-outlined white letters spelling "GASOLINE." Installed on side or back of tank truck.

Tour With Texaco Lettering
1930s (5) 6" $100–150/set
Individual black-outlined white letters spelling "TOUR WITH TEXACO." Installed on back of tank truck.

Bulk Plant Signage

Texaco Farm Lubricants Sold Here
1946–1968 (3) 30" x 42" $200–300
Green porcelain sign with green-outlined white band across bottom. Texaco logo in upper center of green area with black "FARM LUBRICANTS" over red "SOLD HERE" across lower white area.

Texaco Farm Service
1968–1971 (5) 30" x 42" $100–150
White porcelain sign with red border in form of Texaco hexagon logo. Black-outlined Texaco logo with red star and white-outlined green T on star at bottom. Black "TEXACO/Farm Service" inside

logo border.

Texaco Marine Lubricants
1961–1968 (5)   15" x 30" $250–350
White porcelain sign with three-color diagonal band at left. Black/white boats on each of three-color bands above small Texaco logo at upper left. Black-outlined red "TEXACO" above black "MARINE/LUBRICANTS" across sign face.

Texaco Industrial Lubricants
1961–1968 (5)   15" x 30" $250–350
White tin litho sign with three-color diagonal band at left. Black/white trucks and equipment on each of three-color bands above small Texaco logo at upper left. Black-outlined red "TEXACO" above black "INDUSTRIAL/LUBRICANTS" across sign face.

Texaco Marine Lubricants
1968–1971 (5)   15" x 30" $200–300
White porcelain sign with three-color diagonal band at left. Black/white boats on each of three-color bands above small Texaco HEXAGON logo at upper left. Black-outlined red "TEXACO" above black "MARINE/LUBRICANTS" across sign face.

Texaco Industrial Lubricants
1968–1971 (5)   15" x 30" $200–300
White tin litho sign with three-color diagonal band at left. Black/white trucks and equipment on each of three-color bands above small Texaco HEXAGON logo at upper left. Black-outlined red "TEXACO" above black "INDUSTRIAL/LUBRI-CANTS" across sign face.

Texaco Aviation Fuels & Lubricants
1968–1990 (5)   unknown $200–300
White tin litho sign with red band across bottom. Texaco hexagon logo superimposed on red/black "rocket" to left on white area beside black "Aviation." White "FUELS & LUBRI-CANTS" on red area below.

Texaco Marine Products
1946–1968 (5)   24" x 96" $500–750
Red porcelain sign with black band across bottom. Black-outlined white Texaco logo with white-outlined green "T" on red star at either end above

black band, with black-outlined white "TEXACO" between. White "MARINE PRODUCTS" on lower black band.

Texaco Marine Products
1968–1982 (5)   24" x 96" $150–250
White porcelain sign with Texaco hexagon logo at either end. Black "MARINE/PRODUCTS" between logos.

TexGas Sold Here
1968–1970 (5)   16" x 16" $75–100
White-outlined green tin litho sign with white band across bottom. Black and white bottle gas tank with red Texaco hexagon logo on upper green area. Black "TEXGAS/SOLD HERE" below.

Advance Signs
Texaco Ahead
1950–1970 (4)   42" x 84" $75–125
Large white tin litho sign placed along the roadside about a mile ahead of Texaco stations. Red "TEXACO/AHEAD" across sign.

Indian Oil & Refining Co., Lawrenceville, Illinois
Identification Signs
Havoline Service Station
1924–1928 (5)   36" x 45" $600–700
Blue porcelain die-cut sign with blue/white-outlined, red dot circle extending from top of sign. White "HAVOLINE/SERVICE STATION" across center of blue area with red "AUTHO-RIZED DEALER" across bottom of sign.

Indian Gas
1938–1931 (4)   36" x 45" $600–700
Blue porcelain die-cut sign with blue/white-outlined, red dot circle extending from top of sign. White "INDIAN" across top of blue area with white "GAS" offset to right. Small red "INDIAN REFINING CO.,/INCORPORATED" in lower left corner.

Curb Signs
Havoline Waxfree Oil
1930–1935 (5)   12" x 16" $750–850
Blue porcelain die-cut sign with blue/white-outlined, red dot circle extending from top of sign. White "HAVOLINE" across top of blue area above white "WAXFREE OIL."

Airport facilities offering Texaco aviation products were identified by the sign shown here. This example dates from the early 1970s. *Richard Eaves Collection*

Lubricants Signage
Havoline horizontal strip
1920s   (5)   12" x 72" $300–350
Red-outlined, blue porcelain, horizontal-strip sign with white "HAVOLINE" across sign. Red and white concentric circles for "O" in Havoline.

Havoline vertical strip
1920s   (5)   12" x 72" $300–350
Red-outlined, blue porcelain, vertical-strip sign with white "HAVOLINE" vertical down sign. Red dot under "H" and "A" in Havoline.

Havoline, The Power Oil
1920s   (5)   16" x 18" $350–450
Blue porcelain die-cut, flange sign with blue/white-outlined, red dot circle extending from top of sign. White "HAVOLINE" across top of

blue area above white "THE POWER OIL."
California Petroleum Company
Curb Signs
Calpet
1925–1928 (5)   24" x 24" $250–350
Red-bordered, white porcelain sign with white center diamond and black band across center. Black-outlined white "CALIFORNIA PETROLE-UM COMPANY" around border area with red-outlined white "CALPET" on band across center.
Pump Signs
Calpet
1925–1928 (5)   10" x 16" $250–350
Red-bordered white porcelain sign with white center diamond and black band across center. Black-outlined white "CALIFORNIA PETROLEUM COMPANY" around border area with red-outlined white "CALPET" on band across center. White mounting tab and base area with red

One of the most unique signs ever used in the petroleum industry is the Texaco stained glass building insert window. *Richard Eaves Collection*

"GASOLINE" across below diamond.

Paragon Refining Co., Long Island City, New York
Curb Signs
The Paragon curb signs that are known are from the Toledo based independent, and are not in any way related to the Texaco affiliate Paragon.

McColl-Frontenac Oil Co., Ltd., Toronto, Ontario, Canada
Identification Signs
McColl Frontenac Products
1936–1940 (4)   42" $1,500–2,800
Black outline ring around white outer ring. Red and black circle, split diagonal in center of sign inside white ring. Detailed red and black Indian head on white circle in center of red and black area. Black "McCOLL - FRONTENAC" arched around top, "PRODUCTS" around bottom.

Red Indian Gasoline Motor Oil
1940–1947 (4)   60" $1,500–2,800
Black outline ring around white outer ring. Red and black circle, split diagonal in center of sign inside white ring. Detailed red and black Indian head on white circle in center of red and black area. Black "GASOLINE" arched around top, "MOTOR OILS" around bottom.

Pump Signs
Red Indian
1936–1947 (4)   12" $500–650
Die-cut image of detailed red and black Indian head on white circle offset to left of head. No wording appears on this sign.

Caltex: Arabian American Oil Co., New York, New York

Identification Signs
Caltex Carburants Lubrifants
1936–1940 (4)   42"   no listing
Black outline around red outer ring. Black-outlined white circular red star logo in center. Black "CALTEX" across lower center of star. White "CARBURANTS" (i.e., gasoline) arched around top of red band, "LUBRIFANTS" (i.e., lubricants) arched around bottom. Black "MARQUE DE-POSEE" under star.

Caltex
1946–1970s (4)   60" $150–250
Black-outlined white circular sign with large red star in center. Black "CALTEX" across lower center of star.

Pump Signs
Petrol Caltex
1950s   (5)   10"   no listing
Black-outlined white circular sign with large red star in center. Black "CALTEX" across lower center of star, with black "PETROL" arched around top.

In the 1960s, Texaco began marketing a complete line of automotive TBA (Tires, Batteries & Accessories) items. This display promoted Texaco headlights and installation service. *Richard Eaves Collection*

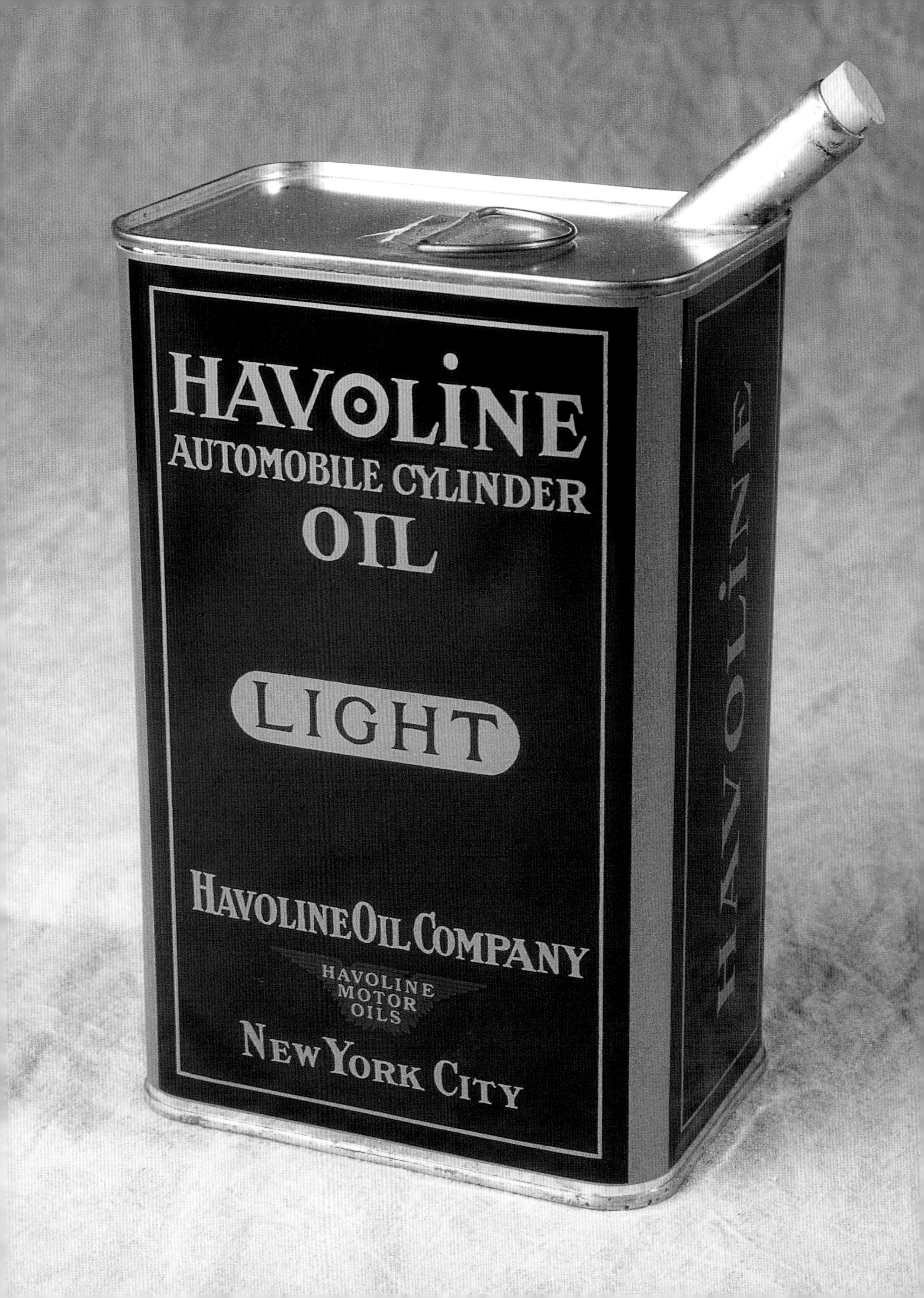

HAVOLINE
AUTOMOBILE CYLINDER
OIL

LIGHT

HAVOLINE OIL COMPANY
HAVOLINE
MOTOR
OILS
NEW YORK CITY

Chapter 6

Texaco Product Containers & Cans

Texaco oil and grease cans have long been popular with collectors, as they are very affordable; many cans can be bought for under $50. These prices, along with the enormous variety of can graphics, make oil cans easy and fun to collect.

Texaco Cans Prior to 1934
From the first Texaco-packaged lubricants before 1910, until the introduction of sealed-quart cans in January 1934, hundreds of Texaco products were packaged in green, lithographed cans of every size and description. While we will not attempt to list all of these containers, they are among the most popular cans with Texaco collectors. The following are some of the highlights of cans from this era.

Earliest cans $50–350
Cans prior to 1915 were light green with a series of black vertical lines on can face. A red-outlined Texaco logo in the center had a red star and black-outlined green "T" with black "PETROLEUM PRODUCTS/HIGH GRADE/UNIFORM QUALITY" across the logo. Most have the product name stamped in a white panel near the top.

Post-1915 cans $50–250
Most Texaco cans in this era had creamy white outlines around green panels on each face. A large

Prior to the purchase of Havoline Oil Company by Indian Refining, Havoline marketed its superior automotive oils in cans like the example shown here. *Richard Eaves Collection*

Other unusual cans include the bulk-grade Texaco "Valor" oil cans used by Texaco in the 1920s and 1930s. *Richard Eaves Collection*

black-outlined white box at the top had the word "TEXACO" above the product name in the box. A red-bordered Texaco logo appeared below the box, with smaller identification or specification text below.

Easy Pour cans, 1920 $150–200
In 1920, Texaco introduced its first motor oil package aimed primarily at the "carry out" market. Before that time much of the motor oil sold was pumped from lubester tanks into glass measuring bottles before being poured into engines. The 1921 introduction of the "EASY POUR" can made carry-out oil popular. The can was round and had a pouring funnel made into the top of the can. The

Texaco "green cans" came in all shapes and sizes for one of the widest assortments of lubricants offered by any petroleum marketer.
Richard Eaves Collection

A very graphic can for the era, this Texaco radiator cleaner can is an extremely rare item from the 1920s.
Richard Eaves Collection

top of the funnel was threaded and sealed with a cap. The cans were green with the black-outlined white box at the top. Black "TEXACO/MOTOR OIL" and the grade name appeared in the box. A larger red-bordered Texaco logo was just below the box, and black text appeared below.

Handy grip cans
1927 $150–200
In 1927, Texaco introduced an unusual can that had a stamped recess on the front and back on one end and a swivel spout connected to the other. To add oil to an engine, you simply removed the

screw cap from the spout, pivoted it around to project out from the can, gripped the can in the hand hold and tilted it as necessary. It carries the same graphics as other Texaco cans of the era, and its use was continued when Clean Clear Golden Texaco Motor Oil was introduced in 1928.

Clean Clear Golden Texaco Motor Oil
1928 $150–200
In 1928, Texaco introduced its "Clean, Clear, Golden Texaco Motor Oil." Package designs remained similar, with the golden-oil pouring can graphic on a black box and all on a large white rectangle added to the traditional green image. These are some of the most beautiful Texaco cans of this era.

Texaco 574 Oil
1932 $35–50
This product was introduced just a few years before sealed quart cans were available. It was packaged in a round quart can slightly smaller in diameter and taller than the later sealed cans. It had a short projecting spout and a threaded cap for closure. The can face had a large, black-outlined white box at the top, with black "TEXACO/574 OIL" inside, and a large red-bordered Texaco logo below. These are perhaps the most commonly found of the Texaco green cans, and the end of an era.

Grease cans $75–100
Texaco grease cans in this era were designed much the same as the other product cans, and their friction lids were printed with a large print of the red-bordered Texaco logo. They are quite appealing.

Automotive Motor Oils After 1934
Texaco Motor Oil
When Texaco introduced motor oils in sealed cans, in about 1934, its primary product was simply branded "Texaco Motor Oil." The can featured a Texaco logo on a red square at the top of the can face on the front, and at the bottom of the can face on the reverse. Alternating white squares formed what collectors have termed the Texaco checkerboard cans. The cans listed below list several of the various revisions to the Texaco Motor Oil brand name that appeared on the cans between 1934 and 1962.

Another rarity is this cone-shaped Texaco radiator cleaner container from the 1910s.
Richard Eaves Collection

Texaco Motor Oil
1934–1935 1qt./5qt. $35–50
Checkerboard can with black-outlined Texaco logo with black-outlined "T" on red fields, and black "TEXACO/MOTOR OIL" on white fields.

New Texaco Motor Oil (black)
1936–1938 1qt./5qt. $35–50
Checkerboard can with black-outlined Texaco logo with black-outlined "T" on red fields, and black "NEW/Texaco/MOTOR OIL" on white fields.

New Texaco Motor Oil (green)
1938–1940 1qt./5qt. $35–50
Checkerboard can with green-outlined Texaco logo with white-outlined "T" on red fields, and green "NEW/Texaco/MOTOR OIL" on white fields.

The checkerboard cans used by Texaco from 1934 until 1962 are some of the most popular Texaco cans readily available to collectors today. The piston wave design replaced the checkerboard design in 1962, and continued in use until 1985. *Richard Eaves Collection*

Texaco Motor Oil Insulated
1940–1947   1qt./5qt. $35–50
Checkerboard can with green-outlined Texaco logo with white-outlined "T" on red fields, and green "TEXACO/ MOTOR OIL" above red "INSULATED" above small, green "AGAINST HEAT AGAINST COLD" on white fields.

Texaco Motor Oil Insulated
1947–1952   1qt./5qt. $25–35
Checkerboard can with white, then green-outlined Texaco logo with white-outlined "T" on red fields, and green "TEXACO/MOTOR OIL" above red "INSULATED" above small, green "AGAINST HEAT AGAINST COLD" on white fields.

Improved Texaco Motor Oil
1952–1959   1qt./5qt. $25–35
Checkerboard can with green-outlined Texaco logo with white-outlined "T" on red fields, and green-outlined white box with red "IMPROVED" above green "TEXACO/MOTOR OIL" on white fields. Corporate name shown as "THE TEXAS COMPANY."

Improved Texaco Motor Oil
May 1959   1qt./5qt. $25–35
Checkerboard can with green-outlined Texaco logo with white-outlined "T" on red fields, and green-outlined white box with red "IMPROVED" above green "TEXACO/MOTOR OIL" on white fields. Corporate name shown as "TEXACO, INC."

Texaco Motor Oil
May 1962   1qt. $25–35
First of the piston-wave cans. Red can with green-outlined white wave across lower can face. White "TEXACO/MOTOR OIL" above green-outlined Texaco logo on red area above wave.

Texaco Motor Oil
Nov. 1962   1qt. $10–25
White can with green-outlined red wave across lower can face. Red "TEXACO/MOTOR OIL" above green-outlined Texaco logo on white area above wave.

Texaco Motor Oil
April 1966   1qt. $10–25
White can with green-outlined red wave across lower can face. Red "TEXACO/MOTOR OIL" above green-outlined Texaco logo on white area above wave. Text revision dated 4/66.

Texaco Motor Oil
Aug. 1967   1qt. $10–25
White can with green-outlined red wave across lower can face. Red "TEXACO/MOTOR OIL" above new hexagonal Texaco logo on white area above wave.

Texaco Motor Oil
Nov. 1968   1qt. $10–25
White composite can with green-outlined red wave across lower can face. Red "TEXACO/MOTOR OIL" above new hexagonal Texaco logo on white area above wave.

Texaco Motor Oil
Jan.1977   1qt. $5–10
White can with red-outlined red wave across lower can face. Large hexagonal Texaco logo above green "MOTOR OIL" on white area above wave.

Texaco Motor Oil
June 1977   1qt. $5–10
White composite can with red-outlined red wave across lower can face. Large hexagonal Texaco logo above green "MOTOR OIL" on white area above wave.

Texaco Motor Oil
Jan.1980   1qt. $5–10
White composite can with red-outlined red wave across lower can face. Small hexagonal Texaco logo above green "MOTOR OIL" on white area above wave.

Texaco Motor Oil
Nov. 1980   1qt., plastic $5–10
White plastic can with green-outlined red wave across lower can face. Red "TEXACO/MOTOR OIL" above new hexagonal Texaco logo on white area above wave. This plastic can, although dated 11/80, reverted to the design introduced in 1967.

Texaco Motor Oil
Oct. 1982   1qt. $5–10
White composite can with red-outlined red wave across lower can face. Large hexagonal Texaco logo above green "MOTOR OIL/HEAVY DUTY" on white area above wave.

Havoline Premium HD Motor Oil
Mar. 1985   1qt. $5–10
With the introduction of the final generation of Texaco cans, the single-grade Texaco Motor Oil became Havoline Premium HD Motor Oil. Solid-black can with new red circle and white star logo above red line near bottom. Gold "Havoline" over red Premium HD" over gold "Motor Oil" across can face above star logo.

Havoline Motor Oil

In 1931, Texaco purchased Indian Refining Company, primarily for access to its superior grade lubricants offered under the Havoline brand. Havoline Motor Oil cans in the 1930s continued to carry the "Indian Refining Company" identification, and even though the title block was changed to read "The Texas Company" before World War II, the word "Texaco" did not appear on any Havoline can until 1958. It was 1962 before the Texaco logo was added to the can design. While rather

Equally as popular as the assorted checkerboard cans are the Havoline "red dot" or "bull's eye" cans used from 1934 until 1962, as well. Many varieties are known, and a complete display can be challenging to find but decorative to display. *Richard Eaves Collection*

plain, the many varieties of Havoline cans make them popular among collectors. All cans prior to 1962 are of the same basic "bull's-eye" design, with a white upper half and blue lower half. Large blue and white-outlined red circle "bull's-eye" logo extends from blue lower area into upper white area. Various text arrangements appear on lower can face, as noted below.

Havoline Motor Oil, Waxfree, Indian Refining
            1qt./5qt. $35–50
Bull's-eye can design with white "HAVOLINE/MOTOR OIL" above red "WAXFREE" on lower can face. Small, white "INDIAN REFINING COMPANY, INCORPORATED" above "ONE U.S. QUART" near bottom of can face. Blue/white "HAVOLINE" vertical down side of can.

Havoline Motor Oil Waxfree Indian Refining
            1qt./5qt. $35–50
Bull's-eye can design with white "HAVOLINE/MOTOR OIL" above red "WAXFREE" on lower can face. Small, white "INDIAN REFINING COMPANY, INCORPORATED" above "ONE U.S.A. QUART" near bottom of can face. Blue/white "HAVOLINE" vertical down side of can.

Unusual Texaco product containers include lubricants for airplanes, diesel engines, transmissions, engine repair work, and other assorted applications.
Richard Eaves Collection

Havoline Motor Oil Distilled And Insulated
   1qt./5qt. $35–50
Bull's-eye can design with white "HAVOLINE/MO-TOR OIL" above small, white "DISTILLED AND" above red "INSULATED" on lower can face. Small-er, white "AGAINST HEAT AGAINST COLD" near bottom of can face. Blue/white "HAVOLINE" vertical down side of can.

Havoline Motor Oil "Keeps Your Engine Clean"
   1qt./5qt. $35–50
Bull's-eye can design with white "HAVOLINE/MO-TOR OIL" above red banner, near bottom of can face. White lettering on red banner reads "KEEPS YOUR ENGINE CLEAN." Blue/white "HAVO-LINE" vertical down side of can.

New And Improved Havoline Motor Oil
   1qt./5qt. $35–50
Bull's-eye can design with white "HAV-OLINE/MOTOR OIL" above red banner, near bottom of can face. White lettering on red banner reads "KEEPS YOUR ENGINE CLEAN." Large, red "NEW AND/ IMPROVED" diagonal at upper left of bull's-eye design. Blue/white "HAVOLINE" vertical down side of can.

Custom Made Havoline Motor Oil
   1qt./5qt. $35–50
Bull's-eye can design with white "HAVOLINE/MOTOR OIL" above red banner, near bottom of can face. White lettering on red banner reads "KEEPS YOUR ENGINE CLEAN." Large red "CUSTOM MADE" diagonal at upper left of bull's-eye design.

Custom Made Havoline Motor Oil
   1qt./5qt. $35–50
Bull's-eye can design with white "HAVOLINE/MO-TOR OIL" above red banner, near bottom of can face. White lettering on red banner reads "HEAVY DUTY." Large, red "CUSTOM MADE" diagonal at upper left of bull's-eye design.

Custom Made Havoline Motor Oil
   1qt./5q $35–50
Bull's-eye can design with white "HAVOLINE/MOTOR OIL" above red banner, near bottom of can face. White lettering on red banner reads "EXCEEDS HEAVY DUTY RE-QUIREMENTS." Large, red "CUSTOM MADE" diagonal at upper left of bull's-eye design.

Advanced Custom Made Havoline Motor Oil
June 1954 1qt./5qt. $25–35
Bull's-eye can design with white "HAV-OLINE/MOTOR OIL" above red banner, near bottom of can face. White lettering on red banner reads "EXTRA HEAVY DUTY." Large, red-out-lined burst with blue script "ADVANCED" above red "CUSTOM MADE" diagonal at upper left of bull's-eye design.

Advanced Custom Made
Havoline Motor Oil A Texaco Product
Sept. 1958 1qt./5qt. $25–35
Bull's-eye can design with white "HAV-OLINE/MOTOR OIL" above red banner, near bottom of can face. White lettering on red banner reads "EXTRA HEAVY DUTY." Large, red-out-lined burst with blue script "ADVANCED" above red "CUSTOM MADE" diagonal at upper left of bull's-eye design. Blue "A TEXACO" to left of bul-l's-eye, "PRODUCT" to right. This was the first time the word Texaco appeared in conjunction with Havoline Motor Oil.

Advanced Custom Made
Havoline Motor Oil A Texaco Product
May 1959   1qt./5qt. $25–35
Bull's-eye can design with white "HAVOLINE/MOTOR OIL" above red banner, near bottom of can face. White lettering on red banner reads "EXTRA HEAVY DUTY." Large, red-outlined burst with blue script "ADVANCED" above red "CUSTOM MADE" diagonal at upper left of bull's-eye design. Blue "A TEXACO" to left of bull's-eye, "PRODUCT" to right. Text revision from 9/58 version.

Havoline Motor Oil
May 1962   1qt. $25–35
First of the "piston wave" design cans. White can with blue-outlined blue piston wave band across lower can face. Blue "HAVOLINE/MOTOR OIL" above blue-outlined Texaco logo on white area above band.

Havoline Motor Oil
Jan. 1963   1qt./1gal $10–25
White can with blue-outlined blue piston wave band across lower can face. Blue "HAVOLINE/ MOTOR OIL" above blue-outlined Texaco logo on white area above band. Text revision dated 1/63.

Havoline Motor Oil
Apr. 1966   1qt./1gal $10–25
White can with blue-outlined blue piston wave band across lower can face. Blue "HAVOLINE/ MOTOR OIL" above blue-outlined Texaco logo on white area above band. Text revision dated 4/66.

Havoline Motor Oil
Aug. 1967   1qt./1gal $10–25
White can with blue-outlined blue piston wave band across lower can face. Blue "HAVOLINE/ MOTOR OIL" above hexagonal Texaco logo on white area above band.

Havoline Motor Oil
Oct. 1968   1qt. $10–25
White composite can with blue-outlined blue piston wave band across lower can face. Blue "HAVOLINE/ MOTOR OIL" above hexagonal Texaco logo on white area above band.

Havoline Motor Oil
Apr. 1971   1qt./1gal $5–10
White can with blue-outlined blue piston wave band across lower can face. Blue "HAVOLINE/ MOTOR OIL" above hexagonal Texaco logo on white area above band.

Havoline Motor Oil
Apr. 1971   1qt. $5–10
White composite can with blue-outlined blue piston wave band across lower can face. Blue "HAVOLINE/ MOTOR OIL" above hexagonal Texaco logo on white area above band.

Texaco Havoline
Jan. 1977   1qt./1gal $5–10
White composite can with blue-outlined blue piston wave band across lower can face. Large hexagonal Texaco logo above blue "HAVOLINE/ MOTOR OIL" on white area above band.

Texaco Havoline
July 1978   1qt./1gal $5–10
White composite can with blue-outlined blue piston wave band across lower can face. Large hexagonal Texaco logo above blue "HAVOLINE/ MOTOR OIL" on white area above band. Text revision dated 7/78.

Texaco Havoline
Mar. 1980   1qt./1gal $5–10
White composite can with blue-outlined blue piston wave band across lower can face. Large hexagonal Texaco logo above blue "HAVOLINE/ MOTOR OIL" on white area above band. Text revision dated 3/80.

Texaco Havoline
July 1981   1qt./1gal $5–10
White composite can with red/blue/red lines forming piston wave band across lower can face. Large hexagonal Texaco logo above blue "HAVOLINE/ MOTOR OIL" on white area above band.

Texaco Havoline
Oct. 1982   1qt./1gal $5–10
White composite can with red/blue/red lines forming piston wave band across lower can face. Large hexagonal Texaco logo above blue "HAVOLINE/ MOTOR OIL" on white area above band. Text revision dated 10/82.

Texaco Havoline
Apr. 1983   1qt./1gal $5–10
White composite can with red/blue/red lines forming piston wave band across lower can face. Large new red circle/white star Texaco logo above blue "HAVOLINE/ MOTOR OIL" on white area above band.

Havoline Premium HD
Mar. 1985   1qt. $5–10
Solid-black can with new red circle and white star logo above red line near bottom. Gold "Havoline" over red Premium HD" over gold "SAE 30" across can face above star logo.

Havoline 10w30 Motor Oils
Havoline Motor Oil Special 10w30
June 1955   1qt./5qt. $25–35
Gold bull's-eye can design with white "HAVO-LINE/MOTOR OIL" above gold "SPECIAL 10W30" on bottom blue area. Large, red-outlined burst with blue script "ADVANCED" above red "CUSTOM MADE" diagonal at upper left of bull's-eye design. Blue "A TEXACO" to left of bull's-eye, "PRODUCT" to right. This was the first time the word "Texaco" appeared in conjunction with Havoline Motor Oil.

Havoline Motor Oil Special 10w30
Sept. 1958   1qt./5qt. $25–35
Gold bull's-eye can design with white "HAVO-LINE/MOTOR OIL" above gold "SPECIAL 10W30" on bottom blue area. Large, red-outlined burst with blue script "ADVANCED" above red "CUSTOM MADE" diagonal at upper left of bull's-eye design. Blue "A TEXACO" to left of bull's-eye, "PRODUCT" to right. This was the first time the word "Texaco" appeared in conjunction with Havoline Motor Oil.

Havoline Motor Oil Special 10w30
May 1959   1qt./5qt. $25–35
Gold bull's-eye can design with white "HAVO-LINE/MOTOR OIL" above gold "SPECIAL 10W30" on bottom blue area. Large, red-outlined burst with blue script "ADVANCED" above red "CUSTOM MADE" diagonal at upper left of bull's-eye design. Blue "A TEXACO" to left of bull's-eye, "PRODUCT" to right. This was the first time the word "Texaco" appeared in conjunction with Havoline Motor Oil.

Havoline Motor Oil 10W30
May 1962   1qt./5qt./1gal $25–35
First of the "piston wave" design cans. Gold can with white-outlined blue piston wave band across lower can face. Blue "HAVOLINE/ALL TEMPERATURE MOTOR OIL" above blue-outlined Texaco logo on white area above band.

Havoline Motor Oil 10W30
Apr. 1966   1qt./1gal $10–25
Gold can with white-outlined blue piston wave band across lower can face. Blue "HAVOLINE/ALL TEMPERATURE MOTOR OIL" above blue-outlined Texaco logo on white area above band.

Havoline Motor Oil 10W30
Aug. 1967   1qt./1gal $10–25
Gold can with white-outlined blue piston wave band across lower can face. Blue "HAVOLINE/ALL TEMPERATURE MOTOR OIL" above new Texaco hexagon logo on white area above band.

Havoline Motor Oil 10W30
Oct. 1968   1qt./1gal $10–25
Gold composite can with white-outlined blue piston wave band across lower can face. Blue "HAVOLINE/ALL TEMPERATURE MOTOR OIL" above new Texaco HEXAGON logo on white area above band.

Havoline All-Temperature Multigrade
Apr. 1971   1qt./1gal $5–10
Gold can with series of white lines around lower can face. Blue "HAVOLINE" over red "SUPER PREMIUM" over blue "ALL TEMPERATURE MULTIGRADE" on upper can face, Texaco hexagon logo superimposed over stripes.

Havoline All-Temperature Multigrade
Apr. 1971   1qt./1gal $5–10
Gold composite can with series of white lines around lower can face. Blue "HAVOLINE" over red "SUPER PREMIUM" over blue "ALL TEM-PERATURE MULTIGRADE" on upper can face, Texaco hexagon logo superimposed over stripes.

Havoline All-Temperature 10W30
Apr. 1978   1qt. $5–10
Blue can with gold-outlined gold piston wave band

across lower can face. Large Texaco logo at top of can face over white-outlined red "HAVOLINE." Smaller gold "ALL TEMPERATURE MOTOR OIL" above larger red "10W30" in center of can.

Havoline All-Temperature 10W30
Apr. 1978   1qt. $5–10
Blue composite can with gold-outlined gold piston wave band across lower can face. Large Texaco logo at top of can face over white-outlined red "HAVOLINE." Smaller gold "ALL TEMPERATURE MOTOR OIL" above larger red "10W30" in center of can.

Havoline Super Premium Multigrade
July 1978   1qt. $5–10
Gold can with blue-outlined blue piston wave design around bottom of can. Blue "HAVOLINE" over red "SUPER PREMIUM" over blue "ALL TEMPERATURE MULTIGRADE" on upper can face, below Texaco hexagon logo.

Havoline Super Premium Multigrade
July 1978   1qt. $5–10
Gold composite can with blue-outlined blue piston wave design around bottom of can. Blue "HAVOLINE" over red "SUPER PREMIUM" over blue "ALL TEMPERATURE MULTIGRADE" on upper can face, below Texaco hexagon logo.

New Fuel Economy Tested
Havoline 10W30
? 1979   1qt. $5–10
Silver composite can with red/blue/red/blue piston wave band across lower can face. Small Texaco hexagon logo at top above small, red "FUEL SAVING FORMULA." Larger blue "HAVOLINE" above red "SUPREME." Smaller blue "MOTOR OIL/API SF/CC" just above wave band, white "SAE 10W30" on blue band below.

New Fuel Economy Tested
Havoline 10W30
July, 1981   1qt. $5–10
Silver composite can with red/blue/red/blue piston wave band across lower can face. Small Texaco hexagon logo at top above small, red "FUEL SAVING FORMULA." Larger blue "HAVOLINE" above red "SUPREME." Smaller blue "MOTOR OIL/API SF/CC" just above wave band, white "SAE 10W30" on blue band below. Text revision on back.

Specialty motor oils were also offered in larger quantity sizes. *Richard Eaves Collection*

New Fuel Economy Tested
Havoline 10W30
Oct. 1982   1qt. $5–10
Silver composite can with red/blue/red/blue piston wave band across lower can face. Small Texaco hexagon logo at top above small, red "FUEL SAVING FORMULA." Larger blue "HAVOLINE" above red "SUPREME." Smaller blue "MOTOR OIL/API SF/CC" just above wave band, white "SAE 10W30" on blue band below. Text revision on back.

Havoline Supreme 10W30
Apr. 1983   1qt. $5–10
Silver composite can with red/blue/red/blue piston wave band across lower can face. New Texaco red circle and white star logo at top above small, red "TEXACO." Large blue "HAVOLINE/SUPREME" in center of can face above red "MOTOR OIL " and blue "SAVES GASOLINE." White "SAE 10W30" on blue band below.

Havoline Supreme 10W30
Apr. 1985   1qt. $5–10
Solid black can with new red circle and white star logo above red line near bottom. Gold "Havoline" over red "Supreme" over gold "10W30" across can face above star logo.

Texaco cans of the 1960s and 1970s displayed the piston wave design. *Richard Eaves Collection*

Some Texaco oils could also be purchased in larger-quantity gallon and five-quart containers. Shown here are two of an assortment of gallon cans used over the years. *Richard Eaves Collection*

Havoline 10w40 Motor Oils
Havoline All-Temperature 10W40
Apr. 1978   1qt./1gal $5–10
Gold can with large Texaco logo at top of can face, blue-outlined blue piston wave band across lower can face. Large, blue "HAVOLINE" below logo above red "SUPER PREMIUM" above blue "ALL TEMPERATURE MOTOR OIL."

Havoline Super Premium 10W40
July 1978   1qt./1gal $5–10
Gold composite can with large Texaco logo at top of can face, blue-outlined blue piston wave band across lower can face. Large, blue "HAVOLINE" below logo above red "SUPER PREMIUM" above blue "ALL TEMPERATURE MOTOR OIL."

Havoline Supreme 10W40
? 1979   1qt./1gal $5–10
Gold composite can with red/blue/red piston wave band across lower can face. Small Texaco hexagon logo at top above small, red "FUEL ECONOMY TESTED." Larger blue "HAVOLINE" above red "SUPREME." Smaller blue "MOTOR OIL" just above wave band, red "SAE 10W40" below. Red "NEW" at upper left of can face.

Havoline Supreme 10W40
July 1981   1qt./1gal $5–10
Gold composite can with red/blue/red piston wave band across lower can face. Small Texaco hexagon logo at top above small, red "FUEL ECONOMY TESTED." Larger blue "HAVOLINE" above red "SUPREME." Smaller blue "MOTOR OIL" just above wave band, red "SAE 10W40" below. Text revision on back.

Havoline Supreme 10W40
Oct. 1982   1qt./1gal $5–10
Gold composite can with red/blue/red piston wave band across lower can face. Small Texaco hexagon logo at top above small, red "FUEL ECONOMY TESTED." Larger blue "HAVOLINE" above red "SUPREME." Smaller blue "MOTOR OIL" just above wave band, red "SAE 10W40" below. Text revision on back.

Havoline Supreme 10W40
Apr. 1983   1qt./1gal $5–10
Gold composite can with red/blue/red piston wave

band across lower can face. New Texaco red circle and white star logo at top above small, red "TEX-ACO." Large blue "HAVOLINE/SUPREME" in center of can face above red "MOTOR OIL " and blue "SAVES GASOLINE." Red "SAE 10W40" below band.

Havoline Supreme 10W40
Mar. 1985   1qt. $5–10
Solid black can with new red circle and white star logo above red line near bottom. Gold "HAVO-LINE" over red "SUPREME" over gold "10W40" across can face above star logo.

Havoline 20W50 Motor Oils
Havoline Super Premium 20W50
Apr. 1978   1qt. $5–10
Gold composite can with large Texaco logo at top of can face, blue-outlined blue piston wave band across lower can face. Large, blue "HAVOLINE" below logo above red "SUPER PREMIUM" above blue "ALL TEMPERATURE MOTOR OIL."

Havoline Super Premium 20W50
Mar. 1980   1qt. $5–10
Gold composite can with large Texaco logo at top of can face, blue-outlined blue piston wave band across lower can face. Large, blue "HAVOLINE" below logo above red "SUPER PREMIUM" above blue "ALL TEMPERATURE MOTOR OIL."

Havoline Super Premium 20W50
Feb. 1984   1qt. $5–10
Gold composite can with blue outlined blue piston wave band across lower can face. New Texaco red circle and white star logo at top above small, red "TEXACO." Large blue "HAVOLINE" over smaller blue "SUPER PREMIUM" in center of can face above red "HIGH PERFORMANCE" above blue "MOTOR OIL" and red "SAE 20W50" above band.

High Performance Havoline 20W50
Mar. 1985   1qt. $5–10
Solid black can with new red circle and white star logo above red line near bottom. Gold "Havoline" over white "High Performance" over gold "20W50" across can face above star logo.

Havoline 5W30 Motor Oils
Havoline Supreme 5W30

Some Texaco dealers opted to sell motor oil from bulk in refillable glass containers. This example dates from the mid-1920s. *Richard Eaves Collection*

Mar. 1985   1qt.   no listing
Solid black can with new red circle and white star logo above red line near bottom. Gold "Havoline" over red "Supreme" over gold "5W-30" across can face above star logo.

Texaco Valor Motor Oil
Valor was Texaco's bulk grade motor oil, pumped from lubesters into bulk containers and lithographed two-gallon containers well into the 1960s. While bearing plain graphics, Valor cans are appealing with their use of blue as their primary color. No quart cans are known.

Texaco Valor Oil
1930s–1941   2gal $25–50
White-outlined area around blue can face. White-outlined red "TEXACO" across top above "VAL-OR" arched above "OIL" in center. Small Texaco logo with black-outlined "T" below center above

Paraffin is, of course, a petroleum by-product, and astute marketers offered the waste product for use in home canning or candlemaking. Shown here are "Texwax" packages through the years. *Richard Eaves Collection*

white-outlined red "MANUFACTURED BY/THE TEXAS COMPANY/U.S.A."

Texaco Valor Oil
1946–1959   2gal $25–50
White-outlined area around blue can face. White-outlined red "TEXACO" across top above "VAL-OR" straight above "MOTOR OIL" in center. Small Texaco logo with white-outlined "T" below center above white-outlined red "THE TEXAS COMPANY/ MADE IN U.S.A."

Texaco Diesel Engine Oils
Texaco D-303 HD Motor Oil
1955–1959   1qt. $25–35
Can has white band around upper half and black band around lower. Black and white lines forming large "D" at top above red "303." White "MO-TOR OIL" above red "HD" and Texaco star logo on lower black band.

Texaco D-303 HD Motor Oil
1959–1960s   1qt. $25–35
Can has white band around upper half and green band around lower. Green and white lines forming large "D" at top above red "303." White "MO-TOR OIL" above red "HD" and Texaco star logo on lower green band.

Ursa Motor Oils
The brand name "Ursa" was introduced on quart packages in the early 1960s. Various Ursa oils were offered, a partial list of which is shown below. These cans have never been very popular among collectors, considering their rather plain graphics and confusing array of products. They are listed here for reference, but no attempt is being made at descriptions of individual cans. Ursa motor oils are among the most popular today among owners and operators of diesel engines, particularly in long haul trucking operations.

Three generations of can designs are known:

1. Can has large abstract "Ursa" covering most of can face. Smaller "Texaco" in space above "rsa" in Ursa. Series of color lines around lower can face with oval in center. Motor oil brand name in oval.
2. Can has large abstract "Ursa" covering most of can face. Smaller "Texaco" in space above "rsa" in Ursa. Series of color lines around lower can face with oval in center. Motor oil brand name in oval above words "MOTOR OIL."
3. White or solid color can with series of contrasting color lines making up piston wave band around bottom. Texaco hexagon logo above motor oil brand name above band. Design used on both steel and composite cans.

UrsaTex
      1qt. $5–10
Blue on white type 1.

UrsaTex
      1qt. $5–10
Wave blue on white type 3.

Ursa S-1
      1qt. $5–10
Red on white type 1.

Ursa LA-3 Motor Oil
      1qt. $5–10
White on green type 2.

Ursa S-3
      1qt. $5–10
Green on white type 1.

Ursa S-3 Motor Oil
      1qt. $5–10
Green on white type 2.

Ursa Super-3
      1qt. $5–10
Red and black on white type 1.

Ursa Super-3
      1qt. $5–10
Wave red and black on white type 3.

Ursa Super-3
      1qt. $5–10
Wave red and black on white composite type 3.

Ursa ED
      1qt. $5–10
Red on white type 1.

Ursa ED Motor Oil
      1qt. $5–10
Red on white type 2.

Ursa ED Motor Oil
      1qt. $5–10
Blue on white type 2.

Ursa ED Motor Oil
      1qt. $5–10
Wave red on white type 3.

Ursa ED Motor Oil
      1qt. $5–10
Wave red on white composite type 3.

Ursa Super Plus
      1qt. $5–10
White on green wave type 3.

Ursa Super Plus
      1qt. $5–10
White on green wave composite type 3.

Other Texaco Motor Oils

Texaco Marine Motor Oil
1935–1940s   1qt./sq. gal   no listing
Green upper and lower bands with white center. Detailed ships and seagulls motif seen on many Texaco marine products. Red "TEXACO" arched above black "MARINE/MOTOR OIL" on center of can face with Texaco logo below. Logo with black border "T."

Texaco Marine Motor Oil
1940s–1960s   1qt.   no listing
Green upper and lower bands with white center. Detailed ships and seagulls motif seen on many Texaco marine products. Red "TEXACO" arched above black "MARINE/MOTOR OIL" on center of can face with Texaco logo below. Logo with white border "T."

New Texaco Airplane Oil
1930s   1qt.   no listing
One of the most graphic Texaco oil cans ever pro-

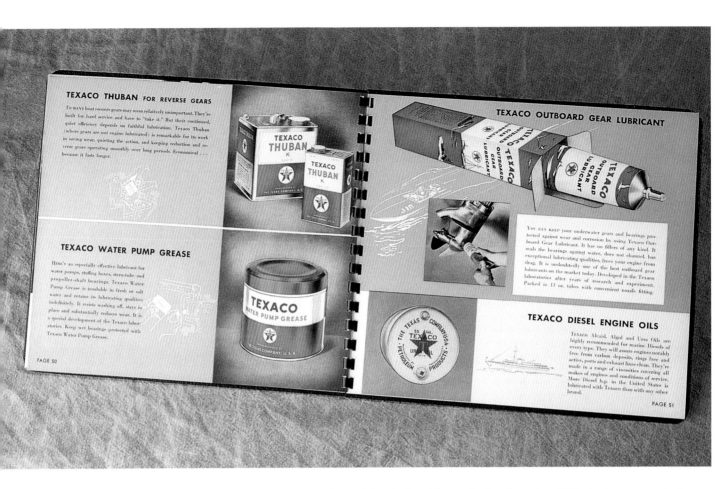

Texaco lubricants were advertised in this guide book. Specialty packaging from the 1930s is shown graphically, giving collectors a "wish-book" to go by! *Richard Eaves Collection*

duced. Similar in design to the marine cans, with a green band across the top and bottom and a white band in the center. Detailed airplanes in the upper green band, with an extremely detailed airport scene across the lower. Black "NEW" above red "TEXACO" above black "AIRPLANE OIL" on upper area of white band, above red-outlined Texaco logo with wings to either side. Fantastic graphics!

Texaco Aircraft Engine Oil
1950s   1qt.   no listing
The early Texaco Aircraft Engine Oil can followed the "checkerboard" design used for Texaco Motor Oil, as well. Green "TEXACO/AIRCRAFT EN-GINE/OIL" on white area, with winged Texaco logo (white border T) on red area.

Texaco Aircraft Engine Oil
1962–1965   1qt. $25–35

White can with red band around base. Texaco logo with red and black "rocket" emblem behind logo at red/white color split. Red "TEXACO" around top, green "AIRCRAFT ENGINE OIL" around bottom of white area.

Texaco Aircraft Engine Oil
1965–1968   1qt. $25–35
White can with green-outlined red "piston wave" band around bottom. Texaco star logo with red and green "rocket" emblem behind logo above wave. Green "TEXACO/ AIRCRAFT/ENGINE OIL" in upper white area.

Texaco Aircraft Engine Oil 10–68
1968–1980   1qt. $10–25
White can with green-outlined red "piston wave" band around bottom. Texaco new hexagon logo with red and green "rocket" emblem behind logo above wave. Green "TEXACO/AIRCRAFT/EN-GINE OIL" in upper white area.

Texaco Aircraft Premium AD 10–68
1968–1980   1qt. $10–25
Gold can with white-outlined red "piston wave" band around bottom. Texaco new hexagon logo with red and black "rocket" emblem behind logo above wave. Black "TEXACO/AIRCRAFT ENGINE OIL/ PREMIUM AD" in upper gold area.

Texaco Aircraft Premium AD
1980s   1qt. $10–25
Gold composite can with red-outlined red "piston wave" band around bottom. Texaco new hexagon logo with red and black "rocket" emblem behind logo at top of can. Black "AIRCRAFT/ENGINE OIL/PREMIUM AD" in upper white area.

Texmatic Fluid
Texaco was among the petroleum marketers who introduced an automatic transmission fluid in quart cans in the early 1950s. The product was called Texmatic Fluid into the 1990s, although specifications were changed to include Dexron, Dexron II, Type F, and others.

Texmatic Fluid
1955   1qt. $25–35
White can with red band around base. Texaco logo centered on red band on can face. Red "TEXACO" above green "TEXMATIC/FLUID" on upper white area above smaller green "AUTOMATIC TRANSMISSION FLUID - TYPE A."

Texmatic Fluid
1959   1qt. $25–35
White can with green band around base. Texaco logo centered on green band on can face. Red "TEXACO" above green "TEXMATIC/FLUID" on upper white area above smaller red "AUTOMATIC TRANSMISSION FLUID - TYPE A."

Texmatic Fluid
1962–1985   1qt. $5–10
We will not be going into details on these cans as they are much less popular than the motor oil cans. In 1962, Texaco adopted a white can with a green-outlined green piston wave band around bottom of can. Similar designs prevailed until the introduction of the black cans in 1985. Product line changes included Texmatic Fluid Type A Suffix A, Texmatic Fluid Dexron, Texmatic Fluid Dexron II, Texmatic Fluid Type F.

Texaco Anti-Freeze
Texaco PT Anti-Freeze
1950s   1qt. $25–35
White can with red band around base. Red "TEXACO" across top above large green "PT." Smaller red lettering amid "PT" to read "PERMANENT" and "TYPE." White "ANTI-FREEZE" above Texaco logo on bottom red band.

Texaco Outboard Motor Oil
Texaco Outboard Motor Oil
1950s   1qt.   no listing
Green glass bottle with white ACL label across center. Red/white/green detailed boats at bottom. White seagulls above label area. Red "TEXACO" above clear (green glass) "OUTBOARD/MOTOR OIL." Texaco logo below above boats.

Texaco Outboard Motor Oil
1946–1959   1qt. $25–35
Rectangular can with radius corners. Green upper and lower bands with white center. Detailed ships and seagulls motif seen on many Texaco marine products. Logo with white border "T."

Texaco Outboard Motor Oil
1959–1962   1qt. $10–25
Rectangular can with radius corners. Green can with white band across top and vertical white rectangle on lower center face area. Red "TEXACO" over green "OUTBOARD/MOTOR OIL" on upper band, large green outboard motor on vertical white area.

Texaco Outboard Motor Oil
1959–1962   1qt. $10–25
Green can with white band across top and vertical white rectangle on lower center face area. Red "TEXACO" over green "OUTBOARD/MOTOR OIL" on upper band, large green outboard motor on vertical white area.

Texaco Outboard Motor Oil
1960s   1qt. $10–25
White can with green-outlined green piston wave around lower can face. Texaco logo at top above red "TEXACO" and green "OUTBOARD/MOTOR OIL" on upper can face above green outboard motor.

Texaco Outboard Motor Oil
1970s   1qt. $10–25
Several versions of cans with purple details and
the new logo are available.

Texaco Home Lubricant
Handy oil cans from all brands have become in-
creasingly popular among collectors in recent years,
providing a great item for display, especially when
collecting from various brands, at relatively low
cost. Early Texaco handy oil cans, branded "Home
Lubricant," are very popular among collectors of
this type of can, with its beautifully detailed graphic
house scene. All Texaco handy oilers except the
newest are hard to find, so enjoy the search.

Texaco Home Lubricant
1920–1934   3oz.   no listing
Early, oval-shaped can with white border around
front and rear green faces. Black-outlined white
box at top of face with black "TEXACO/HOME
LUBRICANT" in box. Red-bordered Texaco logo
in center with black text below. Typical in design
of the early "green cans."

Texaco Home Lubricant
1934–1936   3oz.   no listing
Early, oval-shaped can with red upper half with
black lower half. Red, white, and green suburban
home and neighborhood scene with trees on upper
red area. Green "TEXACO" above white "HOME
LUBRICANT" on black area, above red-outlined
Texaco logo below.

Texaco Home Lubricant
1930s–1940s   4oz. $35–50
One of the most popular Texaco containers. Rectangular can with radius corners. Red upper half
with black lower half. Red, white, and green suburban home and neighborhood scene with trees on
upper red area below Texaco logo. White "TEXA-
CO/HOME/LUBRICANT" on black area below.

Texaco Home Lubricant
1930s–1940s   3oz $50–75
Round can with long, screw-on spout. Red upper
half with black lower half. Red, white, and green
suburban home and neighborhood scene with trees
on upper red area below Texaco logo. White "TEX-
ACO/HOME/LUBRICANT" on black area below.

Texaco Home Lubricant
July 1960   4oz $10–15
Rectangular can with radius corners. White can with
black band around can near top. Texaco logo on
white area above band. White household appliances
on black band. Red "TEXACO" above green
"HOME" above black "LUBRICANT" on lower
white area.

Texaco Home Lubricant
Mar. 1962   3oz $10–15
Round can with long, screw-on spout. Red can with
white-outlined gold "piston wave" band across lower
face. White "TEXACO /HOME/ LUBRICANT"
above green-outlined Texaco logo above band.

Texaco Home Lubricant
Nov. 1967   4oz $5–10
Round can with long, plastic screw-on spout. Red can
with white-outlined gold "piston wave" band across
lower face. Large hexagonal Texaco new logo on upper can face above white "Home/Lubricant" above
band. Part of the "Quality Line" series of products.

Specialty Products
Texaco marketed hundreds of specialty lubricants,
and from the 1930s until the 1962 can re-design, virtually all used variations of the checkerboard design,
with one panel white over green, and the reverse
panel green over white. Some products used
preprinted containers, but many were filled from bulk
and product identification was stamped on the proper panel. Cans of all shapes and sizes were used:
round, square, cap sealed, friction lid, virtually every
design imaginable, suitable for the product contained.
After 1962, the "generic" can was white with a "piston wave" design across the lower face. A Texaco
logo appeared above the band, with a blank area
above or below the logo for product identification.
None of these cans is considered highly collectible, as
there are simply too many of them.

The Quality Line
In the mid-1960s, Texaco finally entered the consumer market arena with a complete line of automotive chemicals, along with some household products.
Never having been overly-involved in these products,
when it made the move to market them, it probably
offered the most complete line possible. No attempt
to list these cans and products will be made, as space

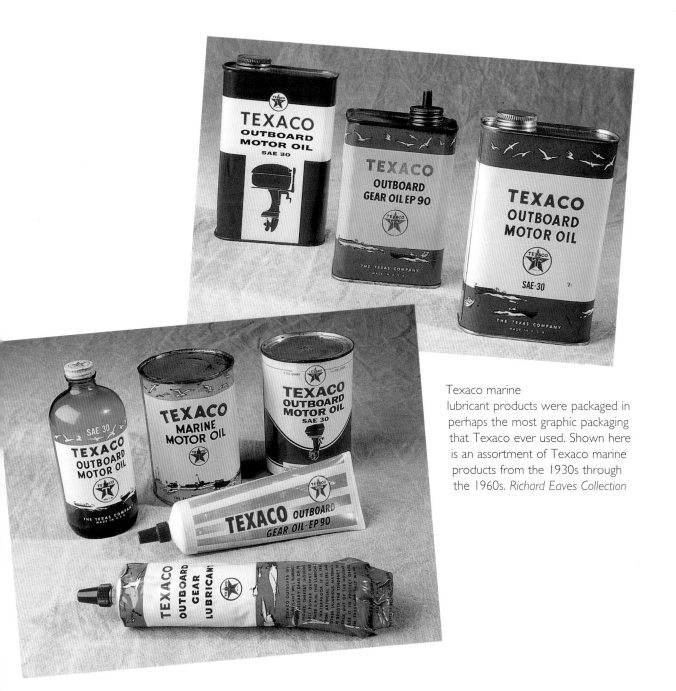

Texaco marine lubricant products were packaged in perhaps the most graphic packaging that Texaco ever used. Shown here is an assortment of Texaco marine products from the 1930s through the 1960s. *Richard Eaves Collection*

is limited and they are not highly collectible. Many interesting can designs exist, though—all of them based on color variations of the "piston wave" design. The marketing effort began before the early logo was removed from containers, and some products are known with the circular logo. With the 1967 addition of the new logo to packaging, the entire product mixture was called "THE QUALITY LINE." Hundreds of products were offered on a regular basis into the 1980s, and many older stations will still have some items on the shelf today.

Chapter 7

Texaco Road Maps and Other Paper Items

Texaco advertising appeared on some early generic maps, but it appears that the first genuine Texaco-branded road maps appeared in 1925. In that year, a series of maps was issued displaying a beautiful, full-color drawing of a motorist and service station attendant beside an open roadster. A gasoline "high-boy" cart is beside the car and a pump with a Texaco globe is in the background. Side panels advertise Texaco gasoline and "Clean, clear, golden" Texaco Motor Oil. It would be over 30 years before Texaco would again offer a map with this much detailed artwork. Texaco maps were mainly very plain in design, but the fact that Texaco was a national marketer that created maps for its entire marketing area adds collectibility, since some 30 different titles were available in the early years.

Texaco road map
1925 $50–75
Full color map with a line drawing of a motorist and service station attendant beside an open roadster. A gasoline "high-boy" cart is beside the car and a pump with a Texaco globe is in the background. Side panels advertise Texaco gasoline and "Clean, clear, golden" Texaco Motor Oil.

Texaco road map
1928–29 $20–25

Although graphically very plain, Texaco road maps of the 1930s are very decorative when displayed in an assortment of styles as shown here.
Richard Eaves Collection

White double-panel map with a line drawing of motorists in an open roadster, parked at a Texaco pump, scanning the latest Texaco map. The motto "TEXACO/ROAD MAP" appeared in red at the top, above the state or area name in green.

Texaco road map
1930–31 $20–25
White double-panel map with a line drawing of a highway scene with a Texaco "Denver" style station in the background. Drawing is in shades of red and green.

Texaco road map
1932 $10–15
White-cover double-panel map. Front cover has green-outlined light green box in center with United States map on box. Texaco logo in compass rose superimposed over map. Red "TEXACO/ROAD MAP" across top above green map title at top. Red band with white "TOUR WITH TEXACO" across bottom. Reverse panel is same.

Texaco road map
1933 $10–15
White-cover double-panel map. Front cover has green-outlined red box in center with United States map on box. Texaco logo in compass rose superimposed over map. Red "TEXACO/ROAD MAP" across top above green map title and date "1933" at top. Red "TOUR WITH TEXACO" across bottom. Reverse panel is same.

In the years before ball-point pens became commonplace, ink blotters were popular advertising giveaways. *Richard Eaves Collection*

Texaco road map
1934 $10–15
White-cover double-panel map. Front cover has blue-outlined green box in center with United States map on box. Texaco logo in compass rose superimposed over map. Red "TEXACO/ROAD MAP" across top above blue map title and date "1934" at top. Red "TOUR WITH TEXACO" across bottom. Reverse panel has Texaco sign and mast arm Denver pole with text.

Texaco road map
1935 $10–15
White-cover double-panel map. Front cover has green/white-outlined red box in center with white "TEXACO" above white script "Road/Map" on box. Texaco logo in compass rose near bottom. Green map title across top and small date in lower right corner. Green script "TOUR WITH" and block "TEXACO" across bottom.

Texaco road map
1936 $10–15
White-cover double-panel map. Front cover has

blue/white-outlined red box in center with white "TEXACO" above white script "Road/Map" on box. Texaco logo in compass rose near bottom. Blue map title across top and small date in lower right corner. Blue script "TOUR WITH" and block "TEXACO" across bottom.

Texaco touring map
1937 $10–15
White-cover double-panel map. Front cover is white with large red box in center and green box below. Green band across top. White-outlined green US map in center of red box with smaller text. Blue "TOUR WITH" above blue-outlined white "TEXACO" in green box. Blue "TEXACO TOURING MAP" in upper green band, above map title in blue. Date in lower right corner.

Texaco touring map
1938 $10–15
White-cover double-panel map. Front cover is white with large red box in center and green box below. Green band across top. White-outlined green US map in center of red box with smaller text. White

"TOUR WITH" above red-outlined white "TEXA-CO" in green box. White "TEXACO TOURING MAP" in upper green band, above map title in green. Date in lower right corner.

Texaco touring map
1939 $10–15
White-cover double-panel map. Front cover is white with large red box in center and green box below. Green band across top. White-outlined very light green US map in center of red box with smaller text. White "TOUR WITH" above red-outlined white "TEXACO" in green box. White "TEXACO TOURING MAP" in upper green band, above map title in green. Date in lower right corner.

Texaco touring map
1940–1945 $10–15
White map cover with green band across top and bottom. White "TEXACO TOURING MAP" in upper green band, small white Text in lower green band. Large Texaco "banjo" sign and pole in center, with map title in green above sign. Most maps were single cover designs, with no reverse, and many titles were not offered during the war years.

Texaco road map
1946–1952 $5–8
White single-cover map with large Texaco banjo sign covering most of map face. Green box at bottom with small white text, red box diagonal across sign pole with white "PAPER IS PREC-IOUS!/PLEASE DO NOT THROW/THIS MAP AWAY." in box. Map title in green at top.

Tour with Texaco
1953–1956 $5–8
Single-cover road map has line drawing of high-way scene with roadside Texaco station in red, white, and blue tones in center. White band across scene at bottom with blue script "TOUR WITH" beside red "TEXACO." Map title in blue at top, small text at bottom.

Tour with Texaco
1957–1960 $5–8
Red double-cover road map with green bands across top and bottom. White cartoon scene of Texaco station at top of red area, and large, full-color Texaco banjo sign image below station to bottom of map.

Black map title in upper green box, white "TOUR WITH TEXACO" above station. Reverse had white box at bottom with "YOUR NEIGHBORHOOD TEXACO DEALER" in box and place to stamp dealer imprint.

Texaco road map
1961–1964 $3–5
One of the most artistic Texaco map covers ever used. Two-cover map with white bands across top and bottom. Upper half of scene shows Texaco station and highway scene, lower half shows Texaco station and downtown city scene. Large banjo sign and pole splits center of both scenes. Red map title at top of both covers, with slogan "TEXACO . . . IN ALL 50 STATES/AND IN CANADA TOO" on lower white block of front, "YOUR NEIGHBORHOOD TEXACO DEALER" and station attendant on reverse white block with place for dealer imprint. Reverse cover for 1962–1964 maps has large advertisement featuring Texaco credit card.

City maps
1961–1964 $3–5
Design is the same as the state maps, but details are printed with scenes in red, white, and blue tones.

Texaco road map
1965–1968 $3–5
Following a trend in the 1960s, Texaco went to a series of "real photo" scenes for its map covers. Scenes varied by state or region, but remained the same throughout the years this design was used. The front cover featured the photo covering most of the cover, with a white band across the bottom. For 1965, 1966, and 1967, the Texaco logo appears in the band, beside the slogan "TRUST YOUR CAR TO THE/MAN WHO WEARS THE STAR." The 1968 map was the first to feature the new logo on the front, in the bottom band beside the slogan "BUY THE BEST...BUY," with "TEXACO" to complete the sentence in the logo. The reverse covers differed every year, with the 1965 and 1966 advertising a Texaco Touring Atlas, 1965 with the slogan "TRUST YOUR CAR TO THE/MAN WHO WEARS THE STAR," at the bottom, the 1966, "DISCOVER AMERICA BEST BY CAR." In 1967, acceptance of the Texaco credit card at Howard Johnson Hotels was promoted on the back cover, along with the Texaco Touring Atlas, then priced at $2.00. For 1968,

the price increased to $3.00. Oddly enough, the credit card shown on the 1967 map shows the new logo, while the rest of the map continues to show the older logo. Phase-in of the hexagon logo was accomplished over a period of several years.

City maps
1965–1968 $2–4
City maps from this era feature a red and blue line drawing of a metropolitan city block on the cover.

Texaco state maps
1969–1970 $2–4
State maps have a white cover with the red, hexagonal border of the new logo repeated three times, one on top of the other. The top one contains the map title in black, the center one a color line drawing of a highway scene, the third with a complete Texaco logo. The reverse displays a credit card, text in black, and a pair of Sky Chief and Fire Chief pumps at the bottom. For 1970, the reverse was modified, with the credit card displayed on a blue background.

Regional maps
1969–1970 $1–2
The front cover of regional maps have only two hexagons, around the map title at the top and the logo below, with the gas pumps pictured below.

City maps
1969–1970 $1–2
The front cover of city maps features a primarily blue city scene, with a red outline hexagon at the top around the map title, and a Texaco hexagon logo at the bottom. Back cover is the same as the state maps.

Texaco road map
1971–1975 $1–2
The front cover of maps from this era features a gold-tone sketch drawing of a Texaco "Matawan" station with a Mustang fastback fueling up in front. The map title appears in black stencil lettering at the top. The reverse, for 1971–74 features a Texaco credit card displayed on a red background. Two different cards appear, the plain one in 1971 through 1972, the graphic one in 1973 and 1974. For 1975, the back cover features an energy conservation message and a single Texaco logo.

City maps
1971–1975 $1–2
The white front cover of the city maps features cartoon drawing of various tourist attractions, with the map title at the top and a hexagon logo at the bottom. The back cover displays a Texaco credit card in a rainbow scene, with text below.

Texaco road map
1976 $3–5
A very small map, with red, white, and blue ribbons near top and bottom, and a small Texaco logo at the lower right. Photos of tourist attractions appear in the center, with the map title in black at the top. The conservation message that appeared on the back of 1975 maps was repeated for 1976.

Texaco road map
1977 $3–5
The last Texaco road map. White map cover with five individual photo scenes on the cover. The map title is in black at the upper left, with special features below in blue. The Texaco logo is at the bottom right.

Specialty Maps
Texaco issued several specialty maps over the years, including marine "Cruising Charts," Travelaide Interstate Maps, Special graphic maps of Washington DC and New York City, and regional "TEXACO Touring Service" maps.

Map Racks
Texaco Touring Service
1935–1952 $35–50
Green lithographed tin map rack with space for single titles only. Multiple racks could be mounted side-by-side for display of several map titles at once. Large, red shield with white "TEXACO/TOURING/SERVICE" on front of rack.

Texaco Touring Service
1952–1968 $25–35
Wire rack designed for multiple titles. White tin litho panel across front of rack with red "TEXACO/TOURING/SERVICE" on panel.

Credit Cards
Credit cards are among the hardest petroleum collectibles to find. Most oil companies began offering branded credit cards in the mid to late-1930s, usually

printed paper cards that were valid for short periods of time, never longer than one year. Many were issued monthly. In the late-1950s, most oil companies replaced their earlier paper cards with plastic or metal plates that could be impress-printed to carbon copy tickets. By 1960, all oil companies—including Texaco—had made the conversion. The plastic cards are much more graphically appealing than the earlier paper cards from most companies, particularly Texaco.

Texaco credit cards
Prior to 1958 $30–50
Texaco credit cards prior to 1958 are often very plain, and although all oil company credit cards are highly collectible, there are no known special graphics or unusual features that make Texaco cards particularly appealing.

Texaco national credit card
1958 $20–25
White plastic embossed card with signature panel, number, customer name and address, and expiration date on white area across bottom. The top has a red/white/green horizontal series of bands across the card with a Texaco logo at the left. On the red band is "TEXACO" in white. On the white band is black "NATIONAL CREDIT CARD/DEALERS IN FORTY-EIGHT STATES AND CANADA." Reverse is entirely text, with no graphics.

Texaco national credit card
1966 $5–10
White plastic embossed card with a one third-width gold band across the top. Large new Texaco hexagon logo centered on gold band. Small black "NATIONAL CREDIT CARD" below band, with embossed number and name below. This card was the first consumer exposure to the new logo.

Texaco travel card
1973 $5–10
In 1973, the 1966 card was modified with the logo shifting to the left. Adjacent to the logo were three picture boxes, matching the small, black description below. Left to right were a car, a boat, and a plane, promoting use of the Texaco card for Texaco products for all kinds of vehicles. The card was renamed the "TRAVEL CARD," which appeared in black just below the logo.

Texaco card
1983 $5–10
Black card face with gray lines forming band across center leading to white star logo and a black star/white "T" at the right. Red "TEXACO" across top of face, with text and the older hexagon logo on the back.

Texaco card
1990 $3–5
The slogan "Star Of The American Road" was added to the top of the gray band in the center.

Note: Other specialty cards and premium cards have been offered over the years.

Calendars
No attempt will be made to list the hundreds of types of calendars to which the Texaco logo has been applied. On the corporate level, many large wall calendars were offered, while on the other end, Texaco distributors were free to purchase calendars from advertising companies and have their custom graphics applied. The "local" nature of some of these makes them very popular with collectors in the respective areas. In the 1940s, Texaco competed with advertising companies by offering a distributor calendar with custom graphics that could be imprinted with the jobber or dealer name. These are perhaps the most commonly found Texaco calendars, and they continue to be popular among collectors.

Matchbooks
No attempt will be made to list the dozens of designs of matchbook covers to which the Texaco logo has been applied. Texaco distributors were free to purchase book matches from advertising companies and have their custom graphics applied. The "local" nature of some of these makes them very popular with collectors in the respective areas. In the 1940s, Texaco competed with advertising companies by offering a distributor specific matchbook with custom graphics that could be imprinted with the jobber or dealer name. These are perhaps the most commonly found Texaco matchbooks and they continue to be popular among collectors.

TO PROVE THAT WE CARE...

...the Texaco Retailer at this Service Station, has personally pledged to Texaco that he will at all times maintain his Rest Rooms as a clean, inviting, sanitary, properly-equipped facility for your convenience and personal comfort.

P.R.A. Huber,
VICE PRESIDENT, SALES U.S.
TEXACO INC

 **TEXACO REST ROOMS LOCKED** *for your protection*

Please **RETURN KEY**

TEXACO *Ladies*

LOCKED FOR YOUR PROTECTION — ATTENDANT HAS KEY

 **TEXACO** *Men*

TEXACO *Men*

TEXACO *Ladies*

LADIES

MEN

Chapter 8

Texaco Rest Room Accessories

Joining other petroleum marketers in the 1930s in realizing that the gas station rest room could be made into a sales tool, Texaco initiated its "Registered Rest Room" program in 1937. Prior to this time, motorists simply had to make do with whatever facilities an enterprising gasoline dealer offered, from the most complete "lounges" in metropolitan stations to a path leading to an outhouse, or the woods, at rural locations. Texaco, more than any other company, changed that image. Texaco Registered Rest Rooms were the company's commitment to the motoring public to provide consistently clean and modern facilities wherever the Texaco sign was displayed.

Keytag board
1940–1967 9" x 12" $75–100
Tin lithographed two-sided sign designed to be placed where it could be viewed through a station window. The back side features a clean rest room pledge in green and white, in a border resembling the "Registered Rest Room" curb sign. The front side is primarily green, with a white band across the top. Black lettering on the band reads "TEXACO/REST ROOMS LOCKED/FOR YOUR PROTECTION." Below that slogan on the green area is a place to hang the two rest room keys.

This collection of Texaco rest room memorabilia illustrates the company's effort toward providing motorists with consistently clean facilities. *Richard Eaves Collection*

Texaco stations participating in the company's "Registered Rest Rooms" program displayed this sign at curbside. *Richard Eaves Collection*

Old logo keytags
1940–1967 $30–35 each
Die-cut tin litho tags designed to appear like Texaco hexagon sign on tapering pole. Black script "Men" or "Ladies" on pole.

Keytag board
1967–1975 9" x 12" $50–75
Tin lithographed two-sided sign designed to be placed where it could be viewed through a station window. The back side features a clean rest room pledge in red and green on white and tan, while the front side has a tan border and white center with a Texaco hexagon logo at the top, over black "REST ROOMS LOCKED/FOR YOUR PRO-TECTION." Below that slogan is a green band with a place to hang the two rest room keys.

New logo keytag
1967–1975 $10–15each
Die-cut tin litho tags designed to appear like Texaco hexagon sign on tapering pole. Black "Men" or "Ladies" on pole.

Rest room comment cards were displayed in these hanging racks. The rest room card rack shown here is from the 1960s. *Richard Eaves Collection*

Chapter 9

Texaco Toys

The Texaco name and image has been applied to thousands of toys, for the benefit of the toy manufacturer, as a promotional by Texaco themselves, and even by collectors of toys for other collectors of toys. The following list includes just a small number of the thousands of Texaco toys produced over the years.

Annual Christmas Promotional Items
Although now a Christmas tradition with virtually every gasoline marketer, Texaco was the first company to offer promotional toys on an annual basis, specifically for Christmas. Beginning in the late-1950s, Texaco has offered some sort of Texaco-branded toy nearly every year, for service station dealers to cash-in on the Christmas toy trade. The following are listings of the toys available through the years.

Texaco pump bank

$175–275

This is thought to be a predecessor to the later Christmas promotional items and dates from about 1954. Detailed cast plastic replica of a short version Tokheim Model 39 gas pump, cast in Fire Chief red, with Texaco Fire Chief decals on each "door." Decals were applied to the dial face, as well. White cast globe is printed with Texaco logo. Bank slot in top,

For collectors young at heart, Texaco offers many different types of toys. Everything—from gas stations to baseballs—is available. *Richard Eaves Collection*

Texaco purchased Paragon Refining in 1959, and for Christmas that year Paragon offered its own version of the Texaco GMC tanker that Texaco retailers offered. Paragon also offered a Christmas 1963 promotional, and by then the Texaco image was beginning to overtake the Paragon brand names. Notice the Texaco decals on the doors. *Richard Eaves Collection*

with bell inside to ring with each coin drop. Detailed hose, nozzle, and setback crank.

1959 Buddy-L GMC Texaco tanker

$250–350

Stock Buddy-L 1958 GMC tractor, painted red and with Texaco decals on each door, pulling a detachable custom designed red tanker trailer. Black-outlined white "TEXACO" up the side of the tanker trailer.

Christmas 1962 saw the introduction of this detailed plastic model of a Texaco ocean-going tanker, the Texaco North Dakota. Employees of Newport News Shipbuilding in Newport News, Virginia, who had constructed the ship, collected hundreds of these models. *Richard Eaves Collection*

Although an oil company branded fire-truck would have been a rare site, seen only in some large refinery complexes, Texaco offered its own version of a "Fire Chief" fire engine for Christmas 1962. *Richard Eaves Collection*

1959 Buddy-L GMC Paragon tanker
no listing
Stock Buddy-L 1958 GMC tractor, painted red and with Paragon shield shaped decals on each door and white "PARAGON/OIL HEAT" decal on the roof, pulling a detachable custom designed green tanker trailer. White "paragon" and a yellow "BUY the BEST/FUEL/OILS" logo up the side of the tanker trailer. Large Paragon shield logo on rear of trailer.

1960 Buddy-L Texaco Station "B.F. Goodrich Tires"
$600–1,200
Detailed lithographed tin model of a typical "Teague" two-bay Texaco station. Complete with front and side pump islands, two Texaco banjo signs, oil racks, signs, cars, and other accessories. Decals in showroom window advertising "B.F. Goodrich" tires.

1960 Buddy-L Texaco Station "Firestone Tires"
$600–1,200
Detailed lithographed tin model of a typical "Teague" two-bay Texaco station. Complete with front and side pump islands, two Texaco banjo signs, oil racks, signs, cars, and other accessories. Decals in showroom window advertising "Firestone" tires.

For Christmas 1963, Texaco retailers offered this Ford version Texaco tanker as a promotional toy. Collectors highly prize these toy trucks today. *Richard Eaves Collection*

1961 Texaco North Dakota

$175–350

Plastic scale model of the Texaco North Dakota, an ocean going tanker launched at Newport News Shipbuilding in the late 1950s. Model is beautifully detailed, an accurate replica of the real ship.

1962 AMF Wen-Mac Texaco fire engine

$250–350

Red painted fire engine on an unpainted base. Detailed plastic fittings in black, chrome, and gold. Detailed cab interior. Texaco logo decal on each door, and gold "TEXACO FIRE CHIEF" along body behind door. Two versions were produced, with extremely minimal differences.

1962 Buddy-L Texaco fire engine

$350–450

Red painted fire engine on an unpainted base. Detailed plastic fittings in black, chrome, and gold. Detailed cab interior. Texaco logo decal on each door, and gold "TEXACO FIRE CHIEF" along body behind door. Two versions were produced, with extremely minimal differences.

1963 Buddy-L Ford Texaco tanker

$250–325

Stock Buddy-L 1962 Ford tractor, painted red and with Texaco decals on each door, pulling a detachable custom-designed, red tanker trailer. Black-outlined white "TEXACO" up the side of the tanker trailer.

1963 Buddy-L Ford Paragon tanker

no listing

Stock Buddy-L 1958 GMC tractor, painted red and with Texaco decals on each door and white "PARAGON/OIL HEAT" decal on the roof, pulling a detachable custom-designed, green tanker trailer. White "paragon" and a yellow "BUY THE BEST/FUEL/OILS" logo up the side of the tanker trailer. Large Paragon shield logo on rear of trailer.

1964 Texaco Gas Pump

$350–500

Formed lithographed steel replica of a Bennett 2000 series gas pump. Painted red, it had an attached white dial face with lithographed decals, a rubber hose and plastic nozzle, and a crank that rolled gallon dial wheels that could be seen through the face. Open back, with shelves inside for toy storage. Large Texaco Fire Chief decal on the lower door panel.

Some of the most detailed and realistic Texaco toys of all time were the model Texaco stations, made of lithographed tin by several different manufacturers for the Christmas 1960 season. *Richard Eaves Collection*

1965 Texaco Fire Chief hat

$150–200

Cast, hard, red plastic hat with attached white shield on front and gold eagle design on top. Red "TEXACO" and "FIRE/CHIEF" lettering on shield with Texaco star and "T" logo in center. Gold microphone under brim of helmet, with battery back in top and speaker mounted behind logo.

Modernized graphics and steerable front wheels (activated by tilting the cab left or right) were features of the 1968 Texaco Jet Fuel Tanker. *Richard Eaves Collection*

Children have always been fascinated with toy gas pumps, and this 1970s Texaco Fire Chief pump, an open-stock plastic toy, was no exception. *Richard Eaves Collection*

1966 Texaco gas pump

$350–500

The Texaco Gas Pump toy storage chest of 1964 was again offered in 1966.

1968 Brown & Bigelow Texaco jet fuel tanker

$225–325

One piece aviation style fuel truck, with white cab and squared red body. White "TEXACO" lettering on side, with small Texaco hexagon on side of cab. Cab tilted to turn front wheels left or right. Black and chrome plastic details.

1970 Wolverine Texaco Station "Service You Can Trust"

$350–500

Lithographed steel Texaco station on a stock brick rancher format. Texaco lettering above window, with green "SERVICE YOU CAN TRUST" above the service bay doors. White plastic gas pumps and sign pole with Texaco hexagon sign.

1973 Wolverine Texaco Station "Three Stars Only"

$350–500

Same as the earlier station, but without motto above the bay doors. Only three stars appear across the service bay area.

1973 Buddy-L futuristic truck

$75–125

Silver Texaco tanker with red futuristic cab. Large Hexagon decals on tanker body.

1973 Cheerleader doll

$45–75

Plastic "action figure" doll in cheerleader's uniform. Boxed set includes other clothing.

1981 Nylint racing truck

$60–100

Large-scale racing car transporter. Details are not known.

1983 Indy car

$45–65

Large, plastic replica of the Texaco Star race car. Friction drive, with new logo decals. Several other examples of similar race cars are known, but no details are available.

Tin-lithographed service stations are very popular among collectors today, and examples that displayed actual brandnames are even more popular. This Texaco station appeared about 1970.
Richard Eaves Collection

1983 Racing truck

$75–125

Ertl steel 1/25–scale tractor trailer, painted white, with decals for the Texaco-sponsored Tom Sneva racing team. Cab and trailer both feature decals with new logos.

Texaco Nostalgic Collector Series

The Christmas promotional tradition was changed somewhat beginning with Christmas, 1984. In that year, Texaco became the first oil company to custom-imprint the Ertl die-cast toy truck banks. The banks had become popular the year before with grocery chains, department store operations, and others, often given away to select customers and not offered at retail to the public. Texaco was unsure of the promotion, and the first several years saw extremely limited production, with toys available only in certain parts of the country. The series was titled "The Texaco Nostalgic Collector Series," and, at first, the models offered were stock Ertl designs custom decorated for Texaco. Several years into the program, Ertl began offering a custom design for Texaco—accurate replicas of early Texaco vehicles. All are highly collectible today, although production runs today ensure sufficient supply for everyone. The series continues to be

Texaco racing activities were commemorated by the Christmas 1983 promotional toys displaying the colors of Texaco's "Tom Sneva Racing Team." *Richard Eaves Collection*

manufactured today, and the Christmas 1996 toy truck bank, a 1949 tilt-cab tanker, has just been released as of this writing.

This series of toy truck banks is manufactured by Ertl and have been available at select Texaco stations every Christmas since 1984. These trucks were largely missed by collectors in the first several years of issue, and, as a result, the earliest ones are very scarce. The following is a listing through Christmas 1996.

1984: Collector Series #1—1913 Model T Ford Van

$1,000–1,200

Created Texaco imaging applied to a stock version of this popular toy truck bank. These were only available in select markets, and is one of the most sought-after gasoline toys ever made.

1985: Collector Series #2—1926 Mack Tanker
$550–675

Created Texaco imaging applied to a stock version of this toy truck bank.

1986: Collector Series #3—1932 Ford Delivery Van

$450–525

Created Texaco imaging applied to a stock version of this toy truck bank.

1987: Collector Series #4—1905 Ford Van
$100–150

Created Texaco imaging applied to a stock version of this toy truck bank.

1988: Collector Series #5—1918 Ford Runabout
$75–125

Created Texaco imaging applied to a stock version of this toy truck bank.

1989: Collector Series #6—1926 Mack Van
$75–100

For Christmas 1959, Texaco introduced their custom-imprinted version of this GMC toy tanker. It contrasted with other generic, open-stock toys by the custom identification and the fact that they could only be purchased through Texaco dealers. *Richard Eaves Collection*

Created Texaco imaging applied to a stock version of this toy truck bank.

1990: Collector Series #7—1930 Diamond T Tanker
$50–65
Accurate Texaco imaging applied to a stock version of this toy truck bank.

1991: Collector Series #8—Horse-drawn tank wagon
$35–40
Accurate Texaco imaging applied to a stock version of this toy truck bank.

1992: Collector Series #9—1925 Kenworth Barrel Truck
$15–25

Accurate Texaco imaging applied to a stock version of this toy truck bank.

1993: Collector Series #10—1939 Dodge Airflow Tanker
$15–25
Accurate Texaco imaging applied to this custom created toy truck bank.

1994: Collector Series #11—1934 Diamond T Tanker
$15–25
Accurate Texaco imaging applied to this custom created toy truck bank.

1995: Collector Series #12—1910 Mack Tanker
$15–25

Offered as an open-stock toy, this Monogram plastic model kit has proved popular with collectors of Texaco memorabilia with Monogram's choice of Texaco graphics for the finished product.
Richard Eaves Collection

Buddy-L offered several versions of Texaco playsets over the years. These date from the 1970s.
Richard Eaves Collection

Accurate Texaco imaging applied to this custom created toy truck bank.

1996: Collector Series #13—1949 White Tilt-Cab Tanker
$15–25
Accurate Texaco imaging applied to this custom created toy truck bank.

Texaco "Wings of Texaco" Collector Series
1992 Texaco #13 Travelair
$200–250
Unofficially produced by a toy collectors club, this model accurately reproduced the Texaco Airplane #13 Travelair Mystery Plane.

1993 #1 1929 Lockheed Air Express
$150–175
First official release in the "Wings of Texaco" series. Accurate reproduction of Texaco Airplane #5.

1994 #2 1932 Northrop Gamma
$30–35
Accurate reproduction of Texaco Airplane #11.

1995 #3 1931 Steerman
$30–35
Accurate reproduction of Texaco Airplane #14.

1996 #4 1940 Grumman Goose
$30–35
Accurate reproduction of Texaco Airplane #30

Independently Produced Toy Trucks with Texaco Branding
Buddy-L Texaco Econoline Van
Circa 1964   no listing
Solid red Buddy-L Ford Econoline van with Texaco logo decals on the doors and Texaco lettering on the side. Apparently a stock item, offered through toy stores, not a custom creation for Texaco.

Ertl Texaco Tanker
1983 $100–175
Ertl 1/25–scale Tractor Trailer Fuel Transport, with a red conventional cab, and a silver tank body with a black square decal offset to rear of tanker body. Large, red circle/white star Texaco logo on black square. New logo decals on cab doors.

Ertl Texaco Tanker 2,000 Image
1988 $40–50
Ertl 1/25–scale Tractor Trailer Fuel Transport, with
a black conventional cab, and a silver tank body
with a black strip decal with red "TEXACO" at
left and the new "white star" logo at right. New
logo decals on cab doors.

Ertl Texaco
Star Of The American Road Tanker
1993 $40–50
Ertl 1/25–scale Tractor Trailer Fuel Transport, with a
black conventional cab, and a silver tank body with
a black strip decal with red "TEXACO" at left and
the new "white star" logo at right. Between is new
slogan "STAR OF THE AMERICAN ROAD" in
red. New logo decals on cab doors.

Monogram 1926 Mack Tanker
1970s $45–60
Stock Monogram plastic model kit that assembled
into a 1926 Mack "bulldog" tank wagon truck.
Featured vintage 1926 Texaco decals to complete
the finished model.

Independently Produced Texaco Stations
Dozens of toy service stations have been produced
with Texaco imaging. No attempt will be made to
list them here, although they are quite popular
among both Texaco enthusiasts and collectors of
gasoline toys in general.

Independently Produced Texaco Pumps
Texaco Fire Chief pump bank
           24" $25–35
Manufactured about 1966, these toy pumps are made
of soft vinyl and are cut in the top for a bank slot.

Texaco Fire Chief pump bank
           18" $25–35
Manufactured about 1966, these toy pumps are
made of soft vinyl and are cut in the top for a
bank slot.

After years of offering Texaco toy trucks at Christmas,
this cheerleader doll was offered in the early-1970s in
an effort to make something available specifically for
motorists with daughters instead of sons.
Richard Eaves Collection

Texaco Fire Chief plastic pump with bell
                             $50–75
Manufactured about 1970, these toy pumps are
made of rigid plastic and feature an outside crank
setback and bell.

Texaco Fire Chief Unleaded plastic pump with bell
                             $50–75
Manufactured about 1975, these toy pumps are
made of rigid plastic and feature an outside crank
setback and bell.

Chapter 10

Texaco Trinkets

Trinkets and giveaways have been a part of Texaco since the 1920s and 1930s. Today these items are relatively easy to collect and remain fairly affordable. Many, like pencils, key chains, and pins, are small and can be easily displayed.

Company-Supplied Trinkets
These items were supplied by Texaco to promote specific products, usually upon introduction, or were given to dealers as prizes for specific product sales achievements. Items, such as the radios, had multiple uses, as they could be sold to anyone, given to favored customers as gifts, or used as dealer or station employee incentives.

Oil Can Banks
Custom Made Havoline Motor Oil
$35–60
A 1940s promotional bank in the image of the "CUSTOM MADE HAVOLINE MOTOR OIL" design, lithographed on a four-ounce-size can.

Radios
Havoline Super Premium All Temperature Motor Oil
$40–50

Over the years, the Texaco name and logo have been seen on just about everything. All these items were either given away or sold to motorists.
Richard Eaves Collection

Texaco advertising trinkets make a nice miniature display, and these items are very popular among collectors. Notice the evolution of graphics shown, and the extremely rare Sky Chief salt shaker from 1956, displaying what was actually advertising from a temporary ad campaign during that year.
Richard Eaves Collection

1971 Promotional radio in the shape of an oil can.

Havoline Supreme Motor Oil
$40–50
1980 Promotional radio in the shape of an oil can.

A.O. Smith Gas Pump - Fire Chief
$65–75

Texaco transistor radios have been offered in assorted designs over the years, promoting various products. Some were sales incentives for specialty products, oil filters, batteries, etc., that were offered to station attendants; others were simply sold as promotional items at Christmastime. *Richard Eaves Collection*

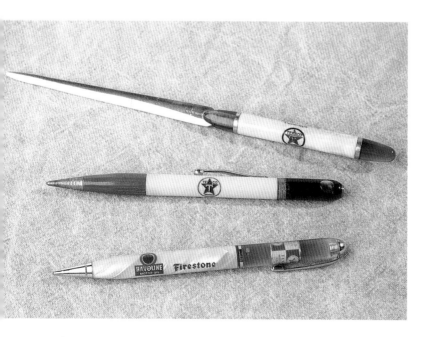

1970s Promotional radio in the shape of an A.O. Smith gas pump labeled for Texaco Fire Chief gasoline.

Tokheim 162 Texaco Super Unleaded Gas Pump radio
$40–50
1980s Promotional radio in the shape of a Tokheim Model 162 gas pump labeled for Texaco Super Unleaded gasoline.

Texaco distributors nationwide used custom-imprinted writing implements to advertise their products. Shown here is an assortment of Texaco pens and pencils from throughout most of this century. *Richard Eaves Collection*

Texaco corporate facilities worldwide, from refinery lunchrooms to the mess halls on Texaco ocean-going tankers, used china emblazoned with the Texaco logo or image. Shown here is an assortment of dishes known to exist today. *Richard Eaves Collection*

Some of the most unusual items of the Texaco place settings are the Texaco flatware displaying the Texaco logo. *Richard Eaves Collection*

Gilbarco MPD radio

$20–30

1990s Promotional radio in the shape of a Gilbarco MPD-1 multi-product gasoline and diesel fuel dispenser labeled for Texaco "System 3" gasoline.

Texaco Oil Filter radio

$35–45

1970s Promotional radio in the shape of a Texaco labeled oil filter.

Texaco Super Chief Battery radio

$75–85

1970s Promotional radio in the shape of an automobile battery and labeled as a "Texaco Super Chief."

Company-Approved Trinkets

Though not supplied directly by Texaco, nor used in conjunction with a particular promotion or product introduction, these items are considered highly collectible today. Manufactured by independent advertising companies and sold through Texaco distributor representatives to independent distributors, these items are often custom imprinted for the dealer or distributor that used them in its own promotions, often tied into station openings or given to heating oil customers as Christmas gifts.

Gas Pump Salt & Pepper Shaker Sets
Texaco Fire Chief and Sky Chief
Pre-1955   (1) $50–100
Red, cast plastic salt shaker labeled in the image of a Texaco Fire Chief Tokheim Model 39 gas pump and a silver, cast plastic salt shaker labeled in the image of a Texaco Sky Chief Tokheim Model 39 gas pump.

Texaco Fire Chief and Sky Chief Su-Preme
1955   (5) $50–100
Same as the earlier set, except the Sky Chief pump is decorated with the image used on a temporary basis when Sky Chief was first called "Su-Preme"

with the introduction of the chemical additive Petrox" in 1955.

Sign Pole Thermometers
Sign pole thermometers were manufactured by Nationwide Advertising Company of Arlington, Texas, and were labeled with the images of virtually every oil company. Individual distributors could buy them with their own custom-printed message on the base. Texaco distributors, of course, were offered this promotion, and many used the thermometers as a gift to their heating oil customers.

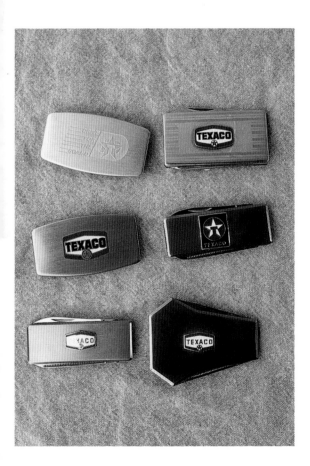

The Texaco logo and image has been applied to pocketknives of all designs over the years.
Some were offered as sales incentives or awards, and some have been made specifically for the collector market.
Richard Eaves Collection

Cigarette lighters are another promotional item that have often been used as sales incentives or awards. Distributors and dealers occasionally used them as customer appreciation gifts, as well. *Richard Eaves Collection*

Belt buckles have become a popular award item in recent years, especially in Texas!
Richard Eaves Collection

Employee badges, often used for identification for access to facilities, or as attendant identification, are eagerly sought after by collectors of Texaco memorabilia. Prices for these items have increased greatly in recent years.
Richard Eaves Collection

Texaco's sponsorship of the 1996 summer Olympics in Atlanta has created many new promotional items that are sure to become collectible. Shown here is an assortment of coffee cups advertising Texaco's ties to the games. *Richard Eaves Collection*

Texaco banjo sign
1950–1968   (2) $25–35
Sign pole thermometer with the image of the classic circular Texaco logo. Custom imprint for local distributors appeared on the pole base.

Texaco hexagon sign
1968–1980   (3) $25–35
Sign pole thermometer with the image of the newer hexagonal Texaco logo. Custom imprint for local distributors appeared on the pole base.

Pens and Pencils
No attempt will be made to list the thousands of types of writing instruments to which the Texaco logo has been applied. On the corporate level, many high-quality pen sets were used as employee incentives, while on the other end, Texaco distributors were free to purchase pens from advertising companies and have their custom graphics applied. The "local" nature of some of these makes them very popular with collectors in the respective areas.

Later uniforms document a change in styles and in company image. This uniform is from about 1970.
Richard Eaves Collection

Texaco attendant coveralls from the 1940s and 1950s. Uniformed attendants gave the impression of authority in automotive service.
Richard Eaves Collection

Employee-Related Items

Uniforms $175–250

Among the many Texaco items that have found popularity among collectors of petroleum memorabilia in recent years are Texaco attendant uniforms. Perhaps the most personal identifier of Texaco service to the motoring public, Texaco attendants at retail stations were attired in a uniform that inferred that the attendant was an authority in meeting the

More Texaco jewelry. Shown here are later Texaco tie-pins. *Richard Eaves Collection*

Texaco jewelry, for identification or award purposes, is highly prized by Texaco employees and collectors of Texaco memorabilia. Shown here are early Texaco tie-pins. *Richard Eaves Collection*

These Texaco tie clips display the 1930s–1960s Texaco logo. *Richard Eaves Collection*

Texaco jewelry, for identification or award purposes, is highly prized by Texaco employees and collectors of Texaco memorabilia. Shown here are Texaco years-of-service award pins. *Richard Eaves Collection*

Another form of Texaco jewelry these early Texaco safety-award pins, which are quite popular with collectors. *Richard Eaves Collection*

Shown here is a Texaco nostalgia collector pin series, issued in Hawaii in the 1990s. *Richard Eaves Collection*

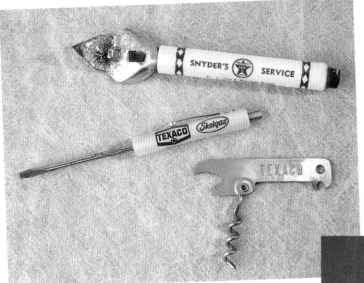

Texaco also imprinted pocket tools, including this bottle opener, screw-driver, and corkscrew. *Richard Eaves Collection*

needs of the motoring public. Several uniform styles are shown in the photos, although no attempt will be made here to describe them. Also popular as collectibles are Texaco attendant hats. Several styles are shown.

Patches $5–25

A part of every Texaco uniform were logo patches. Embroidered emblems representing the Texaco

Texaco fire hats, long symbolic of Texaco Fire Cheif gasoline, have taken many forms as advertising and promotional items. *Richard Eaves Collection*

trademark and special promotional patches are available, in assorted sizes for use on shirt pocket, sleeve, hat, or shirt back. All are highly collectible, although most are commonly found and are available in the $3.00–10.00 range.

Badges $325–500

Prior to the use of embroidered patches, identification badges in several styles were used. Often these badges were made of stamped brass, inlaid with enamel colors, and die cut in the shape of the Texaco logo above an area that a name tag could be inserted. Several designs are known, and these are all very popular among collectors. Some were used as early attendant patches, others as employee passes to corporate facility premises.

Among the many household items to display the Texaco logo are these examples: a calendar and a hand mirror from many years ago. *Richard Eaves Collection*

Coin banks were offered in many forms as Texaco dealer promotionals. *Richard Eaves Collection*

The 1977 celebration of Texaco's 75th anniversary was commemorated by the imitation Tiffany lamp on the left. The popular item was recreated for the jobber-dealer market several years later, displaying the latest logo, as is shown in the example on the right. *Richard Eaves Collection*

HAVOLINE THERMOMETER *A Century of Progress International Exposition* CHICAGO 1934

The Texaco trademark has been displayed on just about every advertising medium ever used. Shown here are various examples. *Richard Eaves Collection*

Dishes $75–250/piece

Found mostly in areas where Texaco operated manufacturing facilities, dishes, glassware, and flatware bearing the Texaco trademark are known. Employee lunchrooms at refineries, lubricants blending plants, aboard offshore drilling platforms, and located on ocean-going tanker ships were the source of these rare and valuable items. No attempt will be made to list them, but several styles are available with various logos used through the years shown.

Texaco's participation in World's Fairs and Expos was often commemorated with numerous advertising items. Shown here are two of several from the 1930s. *Richard Eaves Collection*

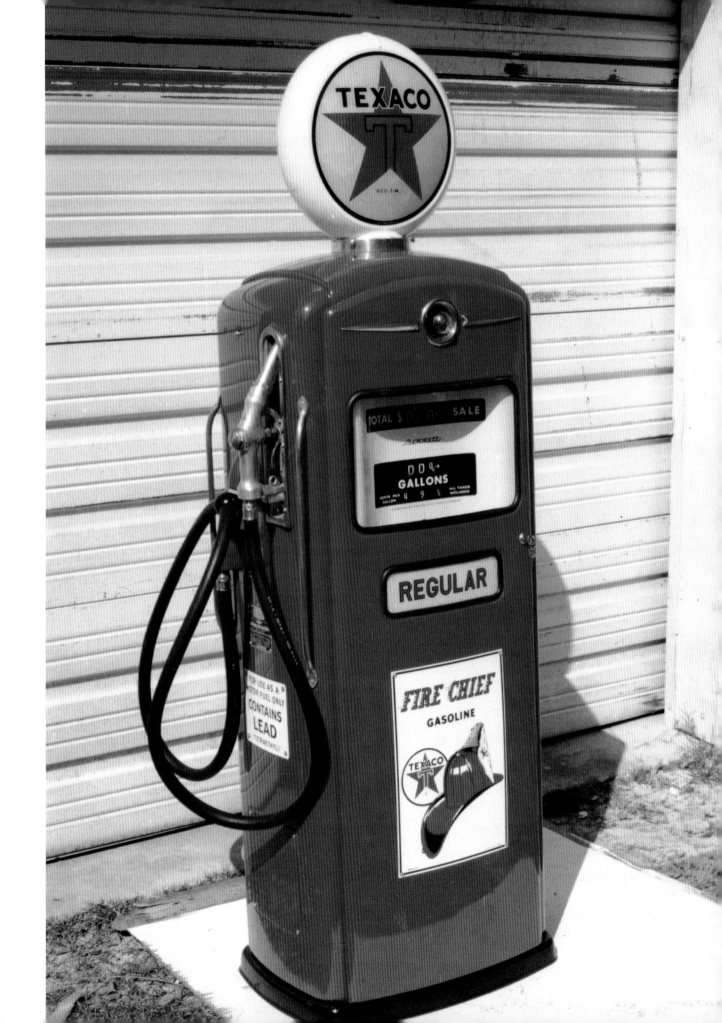

Chapter 11

Texaco Fuels and Gas Pump Color Schemes

In its diverse market, consisting of company stations, jobber stations, dealer stations, country stores, curb pumps, every conceivable method of gasoline retailing, Texaco marketers used every type of pump imaginable, but often specified Tokheim where possible. No Texaco gas pump was ever officially painted green or ever had green trim of any kind. No particular gas pump make was specified to fit any image era. This is partially as a result of Texaco being so jobber-oriented, with equipment purchases handled on a local level. The following color schemes apply to all makes of pumps carrying the brands indicated.

Twin-tank portable lubesters like this unit were used to dispense Texaco motor oil into glass bottles for cars waiting at curbside for lubrication.

Visible and Pre-Visible Pump Era
Regular 1920–1932: Texaco Gasoline
Solid red pump with porcelain Texaco logo sign attached to lower door area. Due to numerous pump styles, flat or round 8" or larger signs may be appropriate.

Regular 1932–1940: Texaco Fire Chief
Solid red pump with several different Fire Chief decals attached to lower door panel. Last decal identical to porcelain pump sign introduced in 1940, except that wording at top read "TEXACO/FIRE CHIEF/GASOLINE."

A collector's restored pump, with the proper globe, but with the use of a central ad glass. The ad glass was virtually forbidden by Texaco image standards.

Premium 1928–1935: Texaco Ethyl
Solid silver pump with Texaco Ethyl decal attached to lower door panel.

Premium 1935–1939: Texaco Fire Chief Ethyl
Solid silver pump with Texaco Fire Chief Ethyl decal attached to lower door panel.

Mechanical Pump Era
Regular 1920–1932: Texaco Gasoline
Solid red pump with porcelain Texaco logo sign attached to lower door area. Due to numerous pump

An unrestored Wayne 70 "diamond in the rough" stands forlornly along a North Carolina roadside.

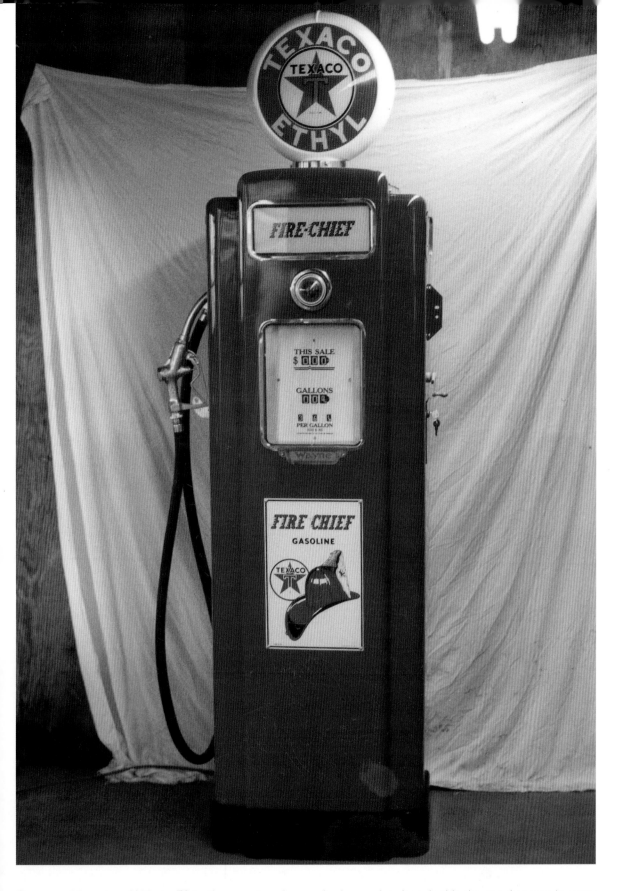

Compare this restored Wayne 70 to the unrestored example shown elsewhere in this chapter. Accurate in every detail except the mis-matched globe displayed atop the pump. This "Fire Chief" image was used from the 1930s until the early 1970s.

styles, flat or round 8" or larger signs may be appropriate. In later years a round Texaco "Clean Clear Golden Motor Oil" sign was attached to the front of pumps.

Regular 1932–1940: Texaco Fire Chief
Solid red pump with several different Fire Chief decals attached to lower door panel. Last decal identical to porcelain pump sign introduced in 1940, except that wording at top read "TEXACO/FIRE CHIEF/GASOLINE."

Premium 1928–1935: Texaco Ethyl
Solid silver pump with Texaco Ethyl decal attached to lower door panel. Several style Ethyl decals are known.

Premium 1935–1939: Texaco Fire Chief Ethyl
Solid silver pump with Texaco Fire Chief Ethyl decal attached to lower door panel.

Motor 1934–1940: Indian
Solid red pump with round "Indian" logo decal attached to lower door panel.

Regular 1940–1972: Texaco Fire Chief
Solid red pump with porcelain Fire Chief pump sign attached to pump above centerline of lower door panel area. On pump designs with ad glass above dial face, ad glasses were used. No ad glass ever used below dial face. Black base.

Premium 1939–1972: Texaco Sky Chief
Solid silver pump with porcelain Sky Chief pump sign attached to pump above centerline of lower door panel area. On pump designs with ad glass above dial face, ad glasses were used. No ad glass ever used below dial face. Black base.

Motor 1940–1949: Indian
Solid red pump with porcelain Indian pump sign attached to pump above centerline of lower door panel area. On pump designs with ad glass above dial face, ad glasses were used. No ad glass ever used below dial face. Black base.

Premium Diesel 1940–1972: Texaco Diesel Chief
Solid red pump with porcelain Diesel Chief pump sign attached to pump above centerline of lower door panel area. No ad glass was used. Black base.

Diesel 1946–1972: Texaco Diesel Fuel #2
Solid bright green pump with porcelain Diesel Fuel #2 pump sign attached to pump above centerline of lower door panel area. No ad glass was used. Black base.

In 1960, Wayne Pump Company manufactured a pair of porcelain-enameled pumps in Texaco red for Fire Chief and a silver-gray for Sky Chief. Shown here is a restored Texaco Fire Chief all-porcelain pump.

Index